英韵李杜美诗①

A Poetry Anthology of Li Bai

by **Li Bai** [Tang Dynasty]
translated by **Xia Han**

李白美诗（汉英对照）

（唐）李　白◎著

夏　晗◎编／译

九　州　出　版　社
JIUZHOUPRESS

图书在版编目（CIP）数据

英韵李杜美诗．1，李白美诗 ：汉英对照 /（唐）李白著 ；夏晗编、译．-- 北京 ：九州出版社，2023.9
ISBN 978-7-5225-2111-4

Ⅰ．①英… Ⅱ．①李… ②夏… Ⅲ．①英语－汉语－对照读物②唐诗－诗集 Ⅳ．① H319.4：I

中国国家版本馆 CIP 数据核字（2023）第 163816 号

英韵李杜美诗①：李白美诗（汉英对照）

作　　者　（唐）李　白 著
译　　者　夏　晗 编／译
责任编辑　周红斌
出版发行　九州出版社
地　　址　北京市西城区阜外大街甲 35 号（100037）
发行电话　（010）68992190/3/5/6
网　　址　www.jiuzhoupress.com
电子信箱　jiuzhou@jiuzhoupress.com
印　　刷　保定市铭泰达印刷有限公司
开　　本　710 毫米 × 1000 毫米　16 开
印　　张　15.5
字　　数　520 千字
版　　次　2023 年 9 月第 1 版
印　　次　2023 年 9 月第 1 次印刷
书　　号　ISBN 978-7-5225-2111-4
定　　价　129.00 元（全二册）

译 序

几年前，笔者选译的唐诗和宋词分别以《美丽唐诗》（汉英双语）、《美丽宋词》（汉英双语）面世后备受赞誉，有人称：“把经典诗词翻译得如此传神到位，不是一般功夫。”有人称“翻译得特别有意境”“翻译得特别美”，等等。这令我备受鼓舞，于是又着手翻译李白和杜甫诗作精选，这就是读者面前的这一套英汉双语《李白美诗》和《杜甫美诗》。

李白和杜甫无疑是中国乃至世界诗歌河汉中的两颗耀眼的巨星，他们的诗歌艺术成就无与伦比，世人对其推崇备至，以至于被分别尊为“诗仙”和“诗圣”，后人将二人并称为“李杜”，二人的诗作备受世人赞誉。唐宋八大家领袖韩愈称“李杜文章在，光焰万丈长”，而唐宋八大家之一、宋代伟大的文学家和词人苏轼则称“李太白、杜子美以英玮绝世之姿，凌跨百代”。和古代的所有知识分子一样，李杜二人心怀崇高政治抱负，以入仕途、安社稷、济苍生为自己的最高政治理想，但时代最终没有赋予他们施展政治抱负的机会，而让他们登上了中国乃至世界诗坛的顶峰。

李白（701 — 762），字太白，是继屈原之后我国又一位伟大的浪漫主义诗人，被世人尊为“诗仙”。一生著作卷帙浩繁，存诗一千多首。在思想内容上，其诗歌反映了其所处时代的社会现实，对统治集团的荒淫和腐败予以无情抨击和批判，表现出对权贵的蔑视和对自由的向往。其诗风豪放飘逸、气势磅礴（杜甫概括为“笔落惊风雷，诗成泣鬼神。”），并且富于奇幻的丰富想象，为世人所崇爱。虽然世人将其与杜甫并成为“李杜”，但后者视其为学长，对其尊崇备至。李白为我们留下的一千余首诗篇已跨越千年，且历久弥新，闪烁着绚烂的思想和艺术光辉，是我们的宝贵精神财富。

杜甫（712 — 770），字子美，唐代伟大的现实主义诗人，被世人尊为“诗圣”。他著作浩繁，一生留下诗歌一千五百余首，其中不少是长诗。在思想内容上，其诗多反映当时的社会现实，特别是民间疾苦，抒发忧国忧民情怀，对朝廷的腐败、社会的黑暗给予揭露和批判，同时也展现了其“致君尧舜上，再使风俗淳”的宏伟抱负。他的诗篇内涵深邃，艺术精湛，炼字精当，格律工整，诗风沉郁顿挫，备受世人推崇，对国内外诗坛产生了深远影响。美国现代诗人雷克斯罗斯认为，杜甫关心人与人之间的爱与宽容，“他是最伟大的诗人，在某些方面甚至超过莎士比亚和荷马。”

李白、杜甫二人诗作卷帙浩繁，对于普通读者来说，不可能倾其全力将其所有两千多首诗歌全部融会贯通。为此，笔者精选翻译两位大诗人的经典名诗各一百首，分别结集为《李白美诗》和《杜甫美诗》，以飨读者。其编选原则为：一是以短诗（律诗、绝句）为主，兼收少量长诗；二是选择名篇，即主要收录两人的代表性名诗。不过，有些虽然属于名篇，但因其过长，不便于读者记诵，只好忍痛割爱。

关于中国古典诗词的翻译策略，不同译者因其翻译观不同，采用的翻译策略也就不同，最终呈现的翻译文本自然也不同。有人喜欢译成格律诗形式，不仅注重原诗内涵的传达，同时考虑诗的韵律——音乐性——的传递；而另一些人则喜欢译成素体诗甚至自由体诗，不追求译文的韵律，只注重原诗内容的表达。至于哪一种方式更好，自然是仁者见仁，智者见智。对此我们应持开放态度，究竟采取哪一种策略，译者自然有选择自主权。

就笔者而言，则倾向于采用格律化翻译策略，既要传递原诗的诗意、诗境和诗情，同时也要再现原诗的音乐特性（声律美），让目标语言读者既领略原诗的深邃文化内涵和意蕴，又体味诗的声律之美。

不过，无论采用哪种策略，都要以译出原诗的意蕴、意境和传达原诗所表达的情感、意趣为要义，也就是要译出原诗的“魂”，不能停留在翻译其字面表层意思。对此，我们不妨以杜甫的《江南逢李龟年》来加以说明。这首诗原文如下：

岐王宅里寻常见，
崔九堂前几度闻。
正是江南好风景，
落花时节又逢君。

诗中的“岐王”是唐玄宗的弟弟李范，崔九即玄宗皇帝的宠臣崔涤，二者是唐玄宗时期王公贵族的两个代表。《江南逢李龟年》绝句的首联回忆在开元盛世之时，诗人和故友李龟年一同出入王公贵族门庭，既反映了当时他们个人的风光荣耀，同时也把开元盛世寓意其中。第二联的“江南”指湖南一带，当时属于比较落后的区域，很多州县是官员遭贬谪后的目的地。“落花时节”暗喻世运的衰颓、社会的离乱，以及漂泊他乡、居无定所的诗人及其友人暮年的衰微与生活的落寞。绝句两联今昔对比，不论是世运，还是个人际遇，与开元盛世已是云泥之别，读了令人内心感到凄楚、伤怀，对诗人及其友人的境遇产生悲悯之情。但是，笔者曾见到过几种版本的译文，读了之后却丝毫体味不到此种感受。

译例一

Meeting Li Guinian in Jiangnan

Often you went to the palace
Of Prince Qi， and then you

Sang again and again for Cui Di;
Jiangnan scenery is now at
Its best; as blossom falls,
So do we meet again.

译例二

Coming Across Li Guinian on the South Shore

In the Qi's residence I'd often the honor to meet you;
In Courtier Cui Jiu's hall I heard you sing for times not a few.
It's now when the beauty of the southern scenery does remain
Except for the fallen flowers that here we meet again.

译例三

Encountering Li Guinian in South

At Prince Qi's mansion a frequent performing guest,
In Cui Jiu's hall you're heard singing your best.
Now at this enchanting time in the southern land,
I meet you again with the flowers falling down to rest.

不难发现，上面三个译例，既有非格律化的译文（译例一），也有格律化的译文（译例二和译例三），但均未能表达出原诗的真谛。事实上，杜甫的这首绝句可被看作唐玄宗时代由盛到衰的一个缩影。

诗人抚今追昔，首联通过回忆与眼前的故友曾一度衣锦出入王公贵族的门庭，也彰示当年的开元之盛；次联写眼下二者已是四处漂泊的天涯沦落人在一个暮春“落花时节”异乡偶遇，暗示昔日盛世不再，整个社会因“安史之乱”已江河日下、衰颓不振。在上述三个译例中，译者各自对首联的翻译大抵比较准确地表达了原文的基本内涵，但次联均未能准确地把经过“安史之乱”后造成的社会凋敝、诗人及其友人李龟年流落异乡的落寞表达出来，反倒像是在赞美此时杜甫与故友相聚时的美丽景色（见译例二），甚至在“促膝赏花”（见译例三），与原诗所表达的惆怅、凄楚和感伤的情境大相径庭。

笔者将杜甫的这首绝句翻译如下：

Coming Across Li Guinian ① in the River-South ②

I used to see you show in Prince Qi's Mansion tall,
And also heard and heard you sing in Lord Cui's Hall.
The River-South's now bathed in the scenery fair,
In th' alien land we meet at the time the blooms fall. ③

这里，将“落花时节又逢君”译为 In the alien land we meet at the time the blooms fall，其中，at the time the blooms fall 具有一定双关意味，既表示“（在）落花时节”，同时也表示“（在）盛世衰

---

① **Li Guinian** a Court musician during the reign of Emperor Xuanzong, and also a friend of the poet.

② **the River-South** here referring to the region covering Hunan and its adjacency.

③ **the time the blooms fall** It not only refers the real situation in which the poet came across his friend Li Guinian, but also a metaphor implying their roving life in a desolate situation, and even the declining Tang Dynasty.

颓的时期”，bloom 除了有“花”的意思外，还有人或事物的“兴盛时期”之义；fall 既表示花的“凋落”，也表示事物的“衰败”。与此同时，把诗中隐含的诗人及其友人漂泊他乡用 in the alien land 译出，暗示二人目前的落寞境遇——二人如今已不再是王公贵族门庭的座上客，而是漂泊异乡的天涯沦落人。此时的江南风景虽美，但两位故友却是“流落异乡为异客，相逢暮春沦落人”，分外悲凉。至于拙译是否贴切地传达了原诗这种意境，恳请读者来品评。

一言以蔽之，译诗一定要抓住原诗的意旨，彰显原诗的意境，传达原诗思想情感，而不能停留在仅仅翻译原诗的基本意思甚至字面表层意思。否则，美国诗人罗伯特·佛罗斯特 Poetry is what gets lost in translation（“译诗所失者，诗也”）的断言岂不真的“一语中的”？

“译诗难，译中国诗更难。”（陆谷孙语）。但是，只要深入思考，潜心探索，亦有道可循。

是为序。

2023 年 7 月 21 日

Preface

I'm so encouraged by the readers' praises, such as "What an exceptional competence of translation to have made the Chinese classical poems so apropos and affectingly expressed (in target language)!" "What an elegant translation!" *et hoc genus omne*, for my English translation of Tang Poetry and Song Verse titled *Fair Tang Poems* and *Fair Song Verses* brought out years ago, that I resolved to translate the poetry gems of Li Bai and Du Fu, bringing forth the books which are now presented to you, the respected readers.

As two giant stars in the arena of poetry in Tang Dynasty (618-907 AD), Li Bai and Du Fu, who are jointly called "Li-Du", have been outshining other poets in both the past and the present, attaining the peak of poetry by right of their numerous poetry works and peerless poetizing artistry. They were highly praised by both their contemporaries and later generations. For example, Han Yu (768-824 AD), the leader of Eight Masters of Tang and Song Dynasties, once aclaimed:

Poems of Li and Du come 'to being,
They, like blaze, are so bright shining.

Su Shi (1037-1101 AD), an outstanding ci-poet of Song Dynasty (960-1279 AD), and also one of Eight Masters once highly applauded the two great poets: "By virtue of their peerless poetry, Li Taibai and Du Zimei have been outliving many a century." Though, like all other intellectuals in ancient China, Li Bai and Du Fu cherished high political aspiration——to engage themselves in the administration of the state's affairs and to contribute themselves to serving the society, the dynasty provided them with no such opportunities to accomplish their political pursuit but had them ascend the acme of poetry.

Li Bai (701-762 AD), also named Li Taibai, another great romanticist poet after Qu Yuan(c.340-278 BC) who was the first romanticist poet in China. He was consecrated as the Immortal of Poets because of his abundance of outshining poetry works (more than a thousand poems) and eminent poetizing artistry. His poems generally revealed the reality of the society in which he lived, criticized the debauchery and corruption of the feudal ruling regime. He also defied the aristocrats and pursued liberty in his lifetime. With majestic air, his poems are sublime and elegant in style, and rich in amazing imaginations, which was, by Du Fu, described as

When his pen touches th'paper, startled are winds and thunders,
Aft his poem's coined, shamed to weep are gods and specters.

His poems are highly admired and praised by generation after generation. Although Li Bai and Du Fu are ever jointly called "Li-Du" by the later generations, Du Fu took Li Bai as a senior scholar and greatly venerated him. Shining with the light of thought and art, his poems have been surviving the ages of more than a thousand years, everlasting and unfading. They are the precious spiritual wealth of not only of Chinese people but also of the whole humankind.

Du Fu (712-770 AD), also named Du Zimei, one of the great

realist poets in Tang Dynasty. He was consecrated as the Sage of Poets because of his voluminous distinguished poetry (over one thousand and five hundred poems) and exceptional poetizing artistry. Like the poetry of Li Bai, Du's poems also revealed the reality of his society, criticized and satirized the darkness and decadency of the reigning regime, as well as showed his sympathy with the suffering and hardship of the poor, expressing his feeling of concerns for the country and the people. Furthermore, many of his poems also reveal his lofty aspiration as shown in one of them:

To 'ssist th' Sovran to outshine Yao and Shun[①] *I incline,*
And 'gain to resume the social ethos pure and fine.

Profound in connotation and excellent in artistry, pathos in style and strict in metrics, as well as precise in diction, Du's poems are greatly appreciated at home and abroad, bringing forth great impact on the arena of poetry in the world. Kenneth Rexroth, a modern American poet, observes that Du's poems are full of love among the people, he was the greatest poet and even exceeded Shakespeare and Homer in some aspects.

As mentioned above, there are numerous poetic works by Li Bai and Du Fu. It is unnecessary for the non-scholar readers to read them through. I selected one hundred poems from each poet's, respectively, to make *A Poetry Anthology of Li Bai* and *A Poetry Anthology of Du Fu* so that the non-scholar readers can read Li Bai and Du Fu without toilsomeness. For the completion of the anthologies, two principles are observed to select the

① Yao and Shun two sagacious emperors in the remote ancient ages of China.

poems: First, the short ones are preferred for their easy recitation. Second, the well-known ones, actually the magnum opuses in which the non-scholar readers are more interested, are preceded to be chosen for these anthologies.

As for the translation strategy for the Chinese classical poems, a different approach is usually adopted by an individual translator in view of his own philosophy of translation. Some prefer to translate them into metrical poems in English, taking account of rhythm and rhyme except for the transmission of sense or connotation of the source texts; others to render them into free verses, mainly taking account of translating the meaning without count of rhythm and rhyme. Which is better? Of course, everyone thinks in his own way. A translator has the right to make his own choice.

I myself prefer the metrical translation approach, trying to make the re-representation of the musicality which stems forth from rhythm and rhyme as well as transmitting the meaning, feeling and appealing of the source poems, so that the readers can comprehend their profound connotation, experience their true affection and appreciate their rhythmic beauty.

It would be a great honour for me if you find the present book helpful for your reading Li Bai and Du Fu so as to understand these two ever-shining great poets and their eternal poetry.

Xia Han

July 21, 2023

目 录

CONTENTS

李　白

（701—762）

静夜思

床前明月光，
疑是地上霜。
举头望明月，
低头思故乡。

Musing in a Still Night

Ere my bed, cast is the moonlight,
I wond'r if be frost on ground it might.
Raising eyes, I gaze at th' moon in shine,
Bending head, for my hometown I pine.

登锦城[①]散花楼[②]

日照锦城头，
朝光散花楼。
金窗夹绣户[③]，
珠箔[④]悬银钩。
飞梯绿云中，
极目散我忧。
暮雨向三峡，
春江绕双流。
今来一登望，
如上九天游。

① 锦城：锦官城的简称，故址在今四川省成都市南。后人用作成都的别称，又称锦里。
② 散花楼：又称锦楼，位于成都摩诃池上，系隋末蜀王杨秀所建。
③ 金窗夹绣户：华丽的窗户和华美的门户。
④ 珠箔：珠帘，用珍珠缀成或饰有珍珠的帘子。

Ascending the Blossom-Scattering Tower ① in Jincheng City

Over th' City ② wall the sun glows,
Bathed in morn light is the Tower ③.
Grand mansion's fixed with fine windows,
Pearl curtains hang on th' hooks silver.
The lofty stairs straight to vaults green ④,
My woe is drowned when I afar look.
On Three Gorges falls the' vesper rain,
The spring river runs 'round th' Twin Brook ⑤.
I now 'scend th' To'er to view the scene
As though I paid a visit to Heav'n.

---

① **Blossom-Scattering Tower** a tower, also called Jinlou Tower which was built in the Mohe Pond, Chengdu at the end of Sui Dynasty.

② **the City** here referring to Jincheng City, nowaday Chengdu, Sichuan Province.

③ **the Tower** here referring to the Blossom-Scatering Tower.

④ **green vaults** referring to the canopies of the trees beside the Tower. The coresspoding expression in the original poem is "green cloud" if literally translated.

⑤ **the Twin Brook** a town located near Chengdu.

峨眉山月歌

峨眉山月半轮秋，
影入平羌[①]江水流。
夜发清溪向三峡，
思君不见下渝州。

① 平羌：平羌江，今青衣江，大渡河支流，位于峨眉山东北。

Song of the Moon over Emei Mountain

Th' autumn cresent o'er Emei Mountain ① is gleaming,
She's reflect'd in the Pingqiang River ② that's surging.
I leave for Three Gorges from the Clear Stream at night,
Sailing to Yuzhou ③, yearning for thee who's out of sight.

---

① **Emei Mountain** or Mount Lady's Brows, located in southwest of nowaday Emei City, Sichuan Province. It has two peaks which look like the brows of a lady —— "Emei" in Chinese——after which the mountain is named.

② **Pingqiang River** also called Qingyi River, a river runs in Sichuan.

③ **Yuzhou** nowaday Chongqing.

渡荆门送别

渡远荆门外，
来从楚国游。
山随平野尽，
江入大荒流。
月下飞天镜[①]，
云生结海楼。
仍怜故乡水，
万里送行舟。

① 月下飞天镜：明月映入江水，如同飞下的天镜。下，向下落。

Sailing for Jingmen Gate①

I sail my boat towards afar Jiangmen Gate,
To make a tour to the ancient Chu State.
Aft hills are passed by, the plain is beheld,
The River' s② flow cleaves the boundless weald.
Like heav'n mirror, the moon alights from skies,
From the rosy clouds the mirages rise.
I love th' riverflow from th' land of my home③,
From 'far it carries my boat to where I come.

---

① **Jingmen Gate** a hill located in nowaday Hubei Province.

② **The River** here referring to the Yangtze River

③ **I love th' riverflow from th' land of my home**. Though Li Bai was not born in Shu, before this journey at about twenty-four, he had been living and studying there since he was five. He lived his childhood and early youth, and took Shu as his hometown ("the land of my home").

江上寄巴东[①]故人

汉水波浪远，
巫山云雨飞。
东风吹客[②]梦，
西落此中时。
觉后思白帝，
佳人[③]与我违[④]。
瞿塘[⑤]饶贾客，
音信莫令稀。

---

① 巴东：巴东郡，指长江三峡的巫峡和瞿塘峡一带。巴东（郡）是唐以前的名称，唐时称信州，诗人这里依然沿用古代名称来指称其挚友（故人）所在地（夔州），诗文中的“巫山”“白帝（城）”“瞿塘”和标题的“巴东”一样，都是用来借指其友人所在地夔州。

② 客：诗人自谓。

③ 佳人：指题中的故人。

④ 违：离别。

⑤ 瞿塘峡：长江三峡之一，位于三峡的巫峡（中段）上游，西入口（即三峡入口），夔州、白帝城均位于这里。

To a Friend in Badong ① from the Hanshui River ②

Afar from thee, surging is the Hanshui River,
Wushan where thou livest cloud and rain loom over ③.
Riding the east wind high in a dream I start
A trip westward and soon arrive at where thou art.
I recall our days in Baidi ④ after I wake,
But now thou and I keep afar separate.
There're traders in Qutang Gorge ⑤ where thou livest,
Allow them to bring me a letter thou shouldest.

---

① **Badong** the ancient name of a prefectural region covering the area of Qutang Gorge and and Wushan Gorge. The poet's friend mentioned in the poem lived in Quizhou located at the entrance of Qutang Gorge, near which Baidi City lies. So the poet used Qutang, Wushan, and Baidi to substitute for the place in which his friend lived.

② **Hanshui River** a the largest branch of the Yangtze River into which the Hanshui River converges in Jiangxia (nowaday Wuchang) where the poet stayed at the time he wrote this poem.

③ **Afar from thee, surging are the Hanshui River, //Wushan where you livest cloud and rain loom over.** These two lines describe the yearning hearts of the two friends——the poet and to whom this poem he wrote——each other for which "the Hanshui is surging" and "cloud and rain loom over Wushan" metephorized. And the poet here used the Hanshui Rirer as a substitution for Wuchang where he lived. Wushan, Wushan Mountain located in Badong (i.e. Kuizhou City) where the poet's friend lived at the time he wrote this poem. Here substituting for Badong.

④ **Baidi** Baidi City, located in nowaday Fengjie County, Chongqing Municipality.

⑤ **Qutang Gorge** one of Three Gorges of Yangtze River located in the Badong Prefecture.

秋下荆门

霜落荆门江树空，
布帆无恙挂秋风。
此行不为鲈鱼鲙，
自爱名山入剡[①]中。

① 剡溪：浙江省绍兴嵊州内的主要河流，由南来的澄潭江和西来的长乐江汇流而成。

Sailing to Jingmen Gate in Autumn

Strand trees have shed their leaves at the frost'd Jingmen Gate,
My sail that's hoist'd in autumn wind is in good state.①
I make this tour not for tasting herring and weever
But come to Shanxi Stream② to enjoy th' hill fairer.

① **The sail that's hoist'd in autumn wind is in good state** It implies that the poet has a good journey.

② **Shanxi Stream** a river located in nowaday Shengzhou, Shaoxing, Zhejiang Province.

望天门山[1]

天门中断楚江[2]开，
碧水东流至此回。
两岸青山相对出，
孤帆一片日边来。

① 天门山：位于今安徽省和县与芜湖市长江两岸。位于江北岸者叫西梁山，位于南岸者叫东梁山（古代又称博望山）。两山隔江对峙，形同天设的门户，故名。

② 楚江：指长江。战国时期安徽天门山所处地域属楚国，故流经这里的长江称作楚江。

A View of Tianmen Mountain①

Tianmen Mountain is cleaved by th' Chujiang Ri'er②,
Green flow eastward runs and takes a turn here.
Th' twin hills twined 'to two sides in scen'ry vie,
A lone sail comes afar from the vast sky.

---

① **Mount Tianmen** the twin mountains located in Wuhu, Anhui Province. They stand by two sides of the Yangtze River, respectively, as if a mountain is cleaved by the River into twins that seem to form a gate through which boats shuttle.

② **Chujiang River** referring to the middle reaches of the Yangtze River located in the ancient Chu State covering Hubei and part of Anhui, here to the Yangtze River.

月夜金陵怀古

苍苍金陵月，
空悬帝王州。
天文列宿在，
霸业大江流。
绿水绝[①]驰道[②]，
青松摧古丘[③]。
台倾鳷鹊观[④]，
宫没凤凰楼[⑤]。
别殿悲清暑[⑥]，
芳园罢乐游[⑦]。
一闻歌玉树[⑧]，
萧瑟后庭秋。

---

① 绝：冲断。

② 驰道：皇道；天子走的道。这里指南朝宋所修的皇宫通往玄武湖的皇道。

③ 古丘：古皇陵。

④ 鳷鹊观：一说鳷鹊观，六朝时所建宫室。

⑤ 凤凰楼：在凤凰山上，南朝宋元嘉年间所建。

⑥ 清暑殿：在台城内，晋孝武帝所建。“虽暑月尤有清风”，故名。（《景定建康志》）

⑦ 芳园罢乐游：在昔日的乐游园里已不见游乐。芳园，即游乐园，在覆舟山南，北连山筑台观，苑内造正阳、林光等殿宇。

⑧ 玉树：陈后主所作《玉树后庭花》，被后人视为亡国的靡靡之音。

Meditation on the Past in Jinling 'neath the Moon

Over Jingling ① the moon sheds her pale light,
Th' royal city seems to float in air in th' night.
The stars still move at their own will in sky,
Gone with torrents has th' past Sovrans' glory.
The royal carriageway's ruined by flood waves,
Withered have th' old pines at th' ancient graves.
Bo'ers in Zhique Palace by now have fallen,
The Pheonix Tower has turned forsaken.
Devoid of joys is the Summer Resort,
Th' Merry Garden's bereft of merry sport.
The Court's drowned in dreary autumn chill,
Though *Court Flower* ② is now and then heard still.

---

① **Jinling** the ancient name of nowaday Nanjing

② ***Court Flower*** a song composed by the Later Emperor of Chen Dynasty. It was believed as a boding tune implying the perishment of a kingdom.

长干行

妾发初覆额，
折花门前剧。
郎骑竹马来，
绕床弄青梅。
同居长干里，
两小无嫌猜。

十四为君妇，
羞颜未尝开。
低头向暗壁，
千唤不一回。

十五始展眉，
愿同尘与灰。

Song of Changgan: A Love Poem

When my hair grew merely to my brow, ①
I used, ere th' gate, to play with picking flo'er.
Riding a bamboo as a horse, come didst thou,
Around th' well we played with green plum 'gether. ②
We both ever dwell in Changgan Alley,
There are no suspicion 'twixt thee and me.

When I was fourteen I was wed to thee,
And shy to 'move my headveil ③ to face thee.
And just lowered my head towards the wall,
And replied not though thou gavest many a call.

When fifteen, I released my knitt'd brows fine,
And I was to knit my heart with thine

---

① **When my hair grew merely to my brow** It implies "When I was a little girl".

② **Riding a bamboo as horse, came come didst thou, /Around th' well we played with green plum together.** In Chinese tradition, "green plum" and "bamboo horse" in these two lines make up a metaphor for their close relationship between a boy and a girl since their childhood, they usually romp together naively as playmate and often become a couple when they grow up.

③ **Headveil** a kerchief that veils the head and face of the bride in Chinese traditional wedding, shying from seeing her looks. Such is an ancient Chinese tradition.

常存抱柱信，
岂上望夫台。

十六君远行，
瞿塘滟滪堆。
五月不可触，
猿声天上哀。

门前迟行迹，
一一生绿苔。
苔深不能扫，
落叶秋风早。

As dust and earth mixed and not twined; I'd rather
Hold the post to die ① than ascend Belvedere. ②

When sixteen, thou madst a long journey
To Qutang ③ in which Yanyu's ④ in the way.
Boat's risky to be on it in th'early summer,
And thou wert also fazed by th' apes' whimper.

'Cause thou on our gate steps treadst rare,
On which mosses overgrow e'erywhere.
The mosses're too dense to clear 'way at all,
The autumn wind blows, having leaves fall.

---

① **Hold the post to die than ascend Belvedere.** According *Zhuangzi*, Weisheng, a young man, made a date with his beloved under a bridge. He waited and waited, but she did not showed up and floods rose. He died with holding a post rather than fled away to break his oath in order to save his life. It is said that he is the first youth who died of love in China. This allusion the poet recited implies the true love will be engraved and praised. It shows that the heroine in the poem so love her husband even lays down her life for love as the eld Weisheng did.

② **Belvedere** a bower built on the high place, for example, on the crest of a mountain, for looking out. Here it refers to a stage at the high place for a wife to looking out (waiting) her husband who left away from home for his career.

③ **Qutang** Qutanag Gorge one of the Three Gorges.

④ **Yanyu** a rock-berg in a river, which is submerged under water when the river tides rise in the early summer. Boats are usually in risk when going by it, especially it is submerged by the tiding flow, becoming a ledge, in the early summer. This line implies that she worried about her husband because of love.

八月蝴蝶来，
双飞西园草。
感此伤妾心，
坐愁红颜老。

早晚下三巴，
预将书报家。
相迎不道远，
直至长风沙。

Butterflies come in th' mid-autumn season,
They fly pair aft pair into th' West Garden,
Which makes me lost into deep mawkishness
And even fade 'way my looks in fairness

Whene'er thou from th' alien land 'turnest,
Thou shouldst write me before thou startest.
I'll pick thee up no matt'r how far is th' way,
E'en if cover thousand a mile it may.

望庐山瀑布二首（其二）

日照香炉[1]生紫烟，
遥看瀑布挂前川。
飞流直下三千尺，
疑是银河落九天[2]。

① 香炉：香炉峰。
② 九天：九重天，指上苍。

A View of the Lushan③ **Waterfall** (Two Poems, No. II)

The Censer② spouts purple smoke③ beneath th' sunny sky,
A waterfall 'far hangs in front of its cliff high
From which thousands of feet falls the rushing water
I wonder if running from heav'n is th' Silver River④.

---

① **Lushan i.e.** Lushan Mountain, also called Kuanglu Mountian or Kuangshan Mountain, a famous mountain located in Jiujiang (the ancient Xunyang), Jiangxi Province.

② **Censer** Censer Peak, a peak of Lushan Mountain.

③ **purple smoke** here referring to the fogs over the mountain peak.

④ **The Silver River** also called Sky River, i.e. the Milky Way in Western culture.

秋夕旅怀

凉风度秋海，
吹我乡思飞。
连山去无际，
流水何时归。
目极浮云色，
心断明月晖。
芳草歇柔艳，
白露催寒衣。
梦长银汉[1]落，
觉罢天星稀。
含悲想旧国[2]，
泣下谁能挥。

① 银汉：银河。
② 旧国：故乡。

Meditation in an Autumn Night during a Tour

The chill autumn winds blow, crossing the brine ①,
It makes it fly 'far th' nostalgia of mine.
On my way, all is mountain aft mountain,
When will the river currents regain?
I look afar, floating clouds heave in sight,
The shining moon has me lost 'to bro'en heart
Green grasses and fair flowers all wither,
White Dew ② urges me to wear cloth warmer.
Of stars' falling from th' Milky Way I dream,
Aft waking, I see only a few stars gleam.
With great woe, I so pine for my hometown
That I can't but shed tears 'long my face down.

---

① **the brine** the sea.

② **White Dew** a solar tem that occurs in midautumnseason from which the weather will becomes chiller and chiller.

雨后望月

四郊阴霭散，
开户半蟾[1]生。
万里舒霜合[2]，
一条江练横。
出时山眼白，
高后海心明。
为惜如团扇[3]，
长吟到五更。

---

① 半蟾：这里指月亮刚从山头升起一半。
② 合：满。
③ 团扇：喻指明月。

A View of the Moon after a Rain

The heavy haze scatters o'er far and nigh,
Through th' windows I see half the moon rise high.
The frost covers thousand miles of weald wide,
A ri'er surges as if floats a ribbon white.
When th' moon just rises, springs spout pale water,
When she hangs high, th' sea becomes a mirror.
To enjoy the moon round-fan-like and bright,
I stay up late to croon poems till th' first light..

上李邕

大鹏一日同风起，
扶摇直上九万里。
假令风歇时下来，
犹能簸却沧溟水。
时人见我恒殊调，
闻余大言皆冷笑。
宣父犹能畏后生，
丈夫未可轻年少。

To Li Yong

With rough a wind the roc is flying high
For myriad a mile towards the vast sky.
If the wind alights on the endless brine ①,
It will make the immense flood decline.
When folks hear my talk out of ordinary,
They might sneer at me for my zealotry.
Even Xuanfu ② paid his esteem to th' young,
Why do Your Excellency look them down?

① **brine** sea.

② **Xuanfu** referring to Confucius who was hallowed as Xuanfu (Father of Xuan) by Emperor of Taizong (Li Shimin) in the 11th year (637 AD) of Zhenguan Period (627—649 AD).

广陵[1]赠别

玉瓶沽美酒，
数里送君还。
系马垂杨下，
衔杯大道间。
天边看渌水[2]，
海上见青山。
兴罢各分袂[3]，
何须醉别颜。

① 广陵：古时扬州的别称。
② 渌水：清澈的绿水。
③ 分袂：挥手告别。袂，衣袖。

Farewell to a Friend in Guangling

The sweet wine is filled in jade jar,
I'll see you off to 'turn afar.
We tether the horse to willow trunk,
Then by road we drink till get drunk
Towards skyline, we see th' green rills,
Across the sea, we 'hold th' blue hills.
We'll part aft drink in merriness,
Why do we care our drunkenness?

金陵酒肆留别

风吹柳花满店香，
吴姬[1]压酒唤客尝。
金陵子弟[2]来相送，
欲行不行各尽觞[3]。
请君试问东流水，
别意与之谁短长？

① 吴姬：吴地的青年女子，这里指酒店里的侍女。
② 子弟：这里指诗人的年轻朋友。
③ 尽觞：喝尽杯中的酒。觞，酒杯。

A Farewell in a Tavern in Jinling City

Balmy in th' tavern while blowing catkins are the winds,
To serve the guests, the maiden of Wu [①] fetches wines.
My young friends in Jinling come to see me off to 'part,
We are all carousing to the full ere I start.
I'd like to beg you to ask th' eastward flowing water:
Which's deeper, my parting woe or th' surging river?

---

① **The maiden of Wu** the maiden of Wu State during the Three Kingdoms Period, here is a substitution for the waitress in the tavern.

金陵城西楼月下吟

金陵夜寂凉风发，
独上高楼望吴越[①]。
白云映水摇空城，
白露垂珠滴秋月。
月下沉吟久不归，
古来相接[②]眼中稀。
解道“澄江净如练”[③]，
令人长忆谢玄晖[④]。

---

① 吴越：古吴和越国，位于今江浙一带。

② 相接：这里指精神相通、心心相印，思想感情上能互生共鸣。

③ “澄江净如练”：谢朓《晚登三山还望京邑》中的诗句。

④ 谢玄晖：谢朓，南朝齐著名诗人，其字玄晖，曾任地方官和京官，受诬陷，死于狱中。

Crooning a Poem in the West Tower in Jinling beneath the Moon

The chill wind blows in Jinling in the still night,
I 'scend the tower to get Wu and Yue' ① s view.
Reflect'd in ripples are th' bleak city and clouds white,
In th' moonlit aut'mn night drops many a clear dew.
Crooning beneath the moon, I loath to return,
So few have had the soulmates e'er since th' ancient.
When reading "Clear is th' ri'er like a sillk ribbon", ②
I'll recall Master Xie③, a shining poet giant.

---

① **Wu and Yue** two ancient states located in nowaday Jiangsu and Zhejiang.

② **Clear is river like silk ribbon** A line from the poem *Looking Back the Capital Aft Ascending Sansham Mountain* by Xie Tiao.

③ **Master Xie** i.e. Xie Xuanhui, also named Xie Tiao, a famous politician and poet in Qi Dynasty during Southern Dynasties,

越中览古

越王勾践破吴归，
义士还家尽锦衣。
宫女如花满春殿[1]，
只今惟有鹧鸪飞。

① 春殿：寓意宫殿充满喜气洋洋的氛围。

Meditation on the Past at the Ancient Capital of Yue State[①]

Goujian[②], th' King of Yue, returned aft beating Wu State[③],
And his warriors came home and dressed in silk attire.
His palace's then bristled with joy and many a maid,
In which now only pattridges fly here and there.

---

① **Yue State** an anient state during Spring and Autumn Period, located in nowaday Zhejiang and Guangdong, taking Huiji (nowaday Shaoxing) as its capital.

② **Goujian** the King of Yue State.

③ **Wu State** an anient state during Spring and Autumn Period, located in nowaday Jiangsu and Anhui.

别东林寺[①]僧

东林送客处，
月出白猿啼。
笑别庐山远，
何烦过虎溪[②]。

① 东林寺：位于庐山的一佛寺。

② 虎溪：庐山的一条溪流。东晋东林寺高僧慧远曾发誓一生不越庐山虎溪，所以诗人不劳其送自己过虎溪（“何烦过虎溪”）。

Farewell to the Monk of Donglin Temple

From Dongling Temple, where I'm sent to depart,
The moon just rises and white monkeys scream.
In smiling, with Monk Master I'll part,
How can I bother him to cross the Tiger Stream[①]?

---

① **How can I bother him to cross the Tiger Stream?** The Monk Master of Dongling Temple, Huiyuan, decided in earlier days to be confined himself to the tiny area around the Donglin Temple and pledged that he would not go farther than Tiger Stream in order to practice dharma. The poet, of course, did not let the Master break His oath just for sending him off. Tiger Stream: a stream near Donglin Temple in Lushan Mountain.

苏台览古

旧苑荒台杨柳新，
菱歌清唱不胜春[①]。
只今惟有西江[②]月，
曾照吴王宫里人[③]。

---

① 不胜春：无尽的美丽春光。
② 西江：从南京以西到江西九江的一段长江，古代称西江。
③ 吴王宫里人：指吴王夫差宫廷里的嫔妃。

Meditation on the Past at Gusu Stage

On th' ruins of garden and bo'er, willows sprouts anew,
Sounds of *Picking Lotus* float amidst the spring hue.
Once gleaming o'er the fairs in th' Palace of Wu's King.
The moon o'er th' West River[①] is now alone shining,

① **West River** in ancient, it referred the Yangtze River, especially to the range of the River from Nanjing to Jiujiang, Jiangxi Province.

夜泊牛渚怀古

牛渚西江[①]夜，
青天无片云。
登舟望秋月，
空忆谢将军[②]。
余亦能高咏[③]，
斯人不可闻。
明朝挂帆席，
枫叶落纷纷。

---

① 西江：从南京以西到江西九江的一段长江，古代称西江。
② 谢将军：东晋谢尚，今河南太康县人，官镇西将军。
③ 高咏：谢尚赏月时，曾闻诗人袁宏在船中高咏，大加赞赏。

Meditation on the Past While Berthing by Niuzhu Hill ① at Night

I've moor'd by Niuzhu Hill on th' West River ② at night,
Without any cloud in sight, 'tis so clear the sky.
Boarding my boat, I gaze at the autumn moon bright,
And 'main recall General Xie ③ with deep a sigh.
I can recite a poem as did his soul mate ④,
Even though my voice he could no longer hear.
Tomorrow I'll set my sail for a leave I take
At the season maple leaves are falling ⑥ here and there.

---

① **Niudu Hill** a mountain located in nowaday Dangtu County, Anhui Provine.

② **West River** in ancient, it referred to the Yangtze River, especially to the range of Yangtze River from Nanjing to Jiujiang, Jiangxi Province.

③ **Gernaral Xie** named Xie Shang, a General of Eastern Jin Dynasty, who once heard Yuan Hong crooned a poem entitled *Ode to History* nearby Niuzhu Hill.

④ **His soul mate** referring to Gernaral Xie's friend named Yuan Yong who then recited a poem which was greatly appreciated by Gernaral Xie.

⑤ **Maple leaves are falling** creating a atomosphere of departure.

山中问答

问余何意栖碧山[①]，
笑而不答心自闲。
桃花流水窅然[②]去，
别有天地非人间。

① 碧山：又称白兆山，位于现湖北省安陆市，山下桃花洞是李白读书处。一说碧山指山色的青翠苍绿。

② 窅然：幽深遥远的样子。

A Dialogue in the Mountain

Inquir'd why I'm secluded in th' hill green,
Without reply, I just smile with serene;
Peach petals on stream are drifting away,
Compare to th' paradise of th' world it may.

黄鹤楼[①]送孟浩然[②]之广陵[③]

故人西辞黄鹤楼，
烟花三月下扬州。
孤帆远影碧空尽，
惟见长江天际流。

① 黄鹤楼：中国著名的名胜古迹，故址在今湖北武汉市武昌蛇山的黄鹄矶上，属于长江下游地带。传说三国时期的费祎于此登仙乘黄鹤而去，故称黄鹤楼。

② 孟浩然：李白的朋友，唐代著名诗人。

③ 广陵：扬州。

Seeing off Meng Haoran ① from Yellow Crane Tower ② to Guangling ③

My friend departs from the Yellow Crane Tower
For Yangzhou in th' late spring full of many a flo'er.
His sail alone fades 'way beneath the azure sky,
I only see the River ④ runs from th' heaven high.

---

① **Meng Haoran** a friend of Li Bai, also a famous poet in Tang Dynasty.

② **Yellow Crane Tower** a tower by Yangtze River, located in Wuchang, Hubei Province.

③ **Guangling** i.e. Yangzhou, Jiangsu Province.

④ **the River** the Yangtze River.

登新平楼

去国登兹楼[①]，

怀归伤暮秋。

天长落日远，

水净寒波流[②]。

秦云起岭树，

胡雁飞沙洲[③]。

苍苍几万里，

目极令人愁。

---

① 兹楼：此楼。

② 寒波流：指泾水。

③ 胡雁：北方的大雁。

Ascending Xinping ① Tower

Far from th' Capital, I ascend this to'er,
In late autumn, I miss home with deep woe.
Th' setting sun yonder hangs low 'neath azure,
The clear currents of chilly River flow.
Haz' clouds arise over the Qinling ② woods,
Swans from th' far north alight on th' bar of sand.
I've been deeply lost into gloomy moods
When 'holding thousand miles of so vast a land.

---

① **Xingping**, a prefecture in Tang Dynasty.

② **Qinling** Qinling Mountain, located Shaanxi Province.

登太白峰

西上太白峰，
夕阳穷登攀。
太白[①]与我语，
为我开天关[②]。
愿乘泠风[③]去，
直出浮云间。
举手可近月，
前行若无山。
一别武功[④]去，
何时复更还？

---

① 太白：太白星，即金星。这里借指天上仙人。

② 天关：《晋书·天文志》："东方，角宿二星为天关，其间天门也，其内天庭也。故黄道经其中，七曜之所行也。"诗人这里指想象中从人间通往上苍的大门。

③ 泠风：轻柔的和风。

④ 武功：这里指武功山，位于今陕西省武功县南约一百里，系太白山的一部分。这里代指太白山（部分代整体）。

Ascending Taibai Peak

I now ascend the Taibai Peak in th' west
Until the sun sets I've not reached its crest.
Where I'm warmly greeted by the Vesper ①
Who, for me, opens th' Heavn Gate ② on higher.
I want to fly by riding th' tender breeze
Up into clouds that are drifting at ease.
Then I can touch the bright moon in the sky
And o'erlook all th' hills as I ahead fly.
I now depart from the Wugong Mountain ③,
When will I on earth come to here again?

---

① **the Vesper** the Venus.

② **the Heavn Gate** the gate to Heaven from the world. Of course, it's a gate the poet imagined.

③ **Wugong Mountain** a mountin located in Wugong County, Shaanxi Province. It is a part of Taibai Mountain.

寄远十二首（其二）

青楼[①]何所在，
乃在碧云中。
宝镜挂秋水[②]，
罗衣轻春风。
新妆坐落日，
怅望金屏[③]空。
念此送短书，
愿同双飞鸿[④]。

① 青楼：豪门显贵家的闺阁。
② 宝镜挂秋水：珍贵的镜子明如秋水。
③ 金屏：华丽的屏风。金，一作“锦”。
④ 飞鸿：飞雁。古代有鸿雁传书的传说。

To Whom Is in Faraway (Twelve Poems, No. II)

Whither can find her gaudy bo'er?
It lies amid the clouds in sky.
Her mirror's much like clear water,
Her silk attires with spring breeze fly.
Dressed in new, she sits in sunset glow,
With woe she's 'lone gazing th' gold screen.
I've swans send her a letter now ①
When haunts my mind all this scene.

① **I've swans send her a letter now** In Chinese myth, a swan can send a letter to a person, especially a lover.

乌栖曲

姑苏台上乌栖时，
吴王宫里醉西施。
吴歌楚舞欢未毕，
青山欲衔半边日。
银箭金壶漏水多，
起看秋月坠江波。
东方渐高奈乐何！

When Crows Perch

When on the Gusu Tower perch crows ①,
Ranee Xishi ② is feasted in Palace by th' King.
Still going on are th' singing and dancing shows
Till mountains have mouthed the sun beaming.
Out of th' gold clepsydra so much water flows,
Into the ripples th' autumn moon seems to fall,
Th' King cares not if it's been dawning at all!

---

① **When on the Gusu Tower perch crows** It means the time in which the below-mentiond feast is hostedin the night when crows have perched in hteir nest for resting.

② **Ranee Xishi** a stunning fair, durig Spring and Autumn Period, who became the ranee of the King of Wu State, Fuchai.

关山月

明月出天山，
苍茫云海间。
长风几万里，
吹度玉门关。
汉下白登道，
胡窥青海湾。
由来征战地，
不见有人还。
戍客望边色，
思归多苦颜。
高楼当此夜，
叹息未应闲。

The Moon over Frontier Mountain

From Tianshan Mountain ① rises the moon bright
As if she were floating ’mid clouds in flight.
High winds blow thousands of miles in th’ vast air,
Passing Yumen Gate ② in th’ northwest frontier.
Once th’ troops of Han marched along th’ Baideng ③ Way,
To fight Tartars who covet th’ Qinghai Bay ④.
None of men who went to the battlefield
Could have returnéd alive since the eld.
When he gazes the stretching frontier’s dreary hue,
A soldier pines for home with knitted brow.
His wife must sigh tonight in her bower,
Craving for his return from the frontier.

---

① **Tianshan Mountain** i.e. Qilian Mountain that lies in Northwest China.

② **Yumen Gate** a pass located in Northwest China.

③ **Baideng** Baideng Mountain.

④ **Qinghai Bay** Qinghai Lake.

友人会宿

涤荡千古愁，
留连百壶饮。
良宵宜清谈，
皓月未能寝。
醉来卧空山，
天地即衾枕。

Staying a Night with a Friend in Mountain

To drown our e'er-haunting grave pine[①],
We'd carouse thousand cups of wine.
We talk'd and talk'd during the night,
And kept sleepless 'neath the noon bright.
Ta'ing heav'n as quilt and earth as bunk,
We lie in th' void mountain aft drunk.

---

① **pine** sadness, sorrow.

玉阶怨

玉阶生白露，
夜久侵罗袜。
却下水精帘，
玲珑望秋月。

Feeling Resentment at the Marble Steps

On th' marble steps arise th' dews white
Which wets her silk socks in th' late night.
Back her room she pulls th' cryst'l screen down,
Alone gazing th' autumn moon bright.

大堤[①]曲

汉水临襄阳，
花开大堤暖。
佳期大堤下，
泪向南云满。
春风复无情，
吹我梦魂散。
不见眼中人，
天长音信断。

---

① 大堤：唐代位于襄阳府城外的大堤坝。

Song of Grand Dyke

Xiangyang City lies by th' Hanshui River,
Th' dyke's warm with many a blooming flower.
When recalling our dates by the dykesides,
I shed my tears, gazing clouds in south skies.
Affectionless is the wind in th' spring day,
'Tis so cruel to blow my love dream away.
My beloved still is out of sight, and I
Hear not from her because of far cry.

襄阳曲四首（其三）

岘山临汉水，
水绿沙如雪。
上有堕泪碑，
青苔久磨灭。

Songs of Xiangyang (Four Poems, No. III)

Xianshan Hill lies by the Hanshui River
In which green is flow and snow-white are sands
On th' Hill, the Monument of Yanghu stands,
On which the scripts are by thick moss cover'd.

江夏[1]别宋之悌

楚水[2]清若空，
遥将[3]碧海通。
人分千里外，
兴在一杯中。
谷鸟吟晴日，
江猿啸晚风。
平生不下泪，
于此泣无穷。

① 江夏：唐代县名，今武昌。
② 楚水：唐诗中经常说的“楚江”，位于古楚国（今湖北）的长江段。
③ 将：与。

Farewell to Song Zhiti in Jianxia City ①

So clear to see th' bottom is th' Chujiang River ②,
That flows afar, straight into the vast brine ③.
You'll leave for where's thousand miles of yonder,
Our friendship is 'yond words but deep in wine.
In sunn' day birds in vale constant twitter,
Against the dusk wind, monkeys ceaseless cry.
During my lifetime I seldom whimper,
But now shedding tears down my face am I.

---

① **Jiangxia** the nowaday Wuchang, Hubei Province.

② **Chujiang River** here is a substitution for Jiangxia, a city by the River.

③ **brine** sea.

江夏[1]送友人

雪点翠云裘[2]，
送君黄鹤楼。
黄鹤振玉羽，
西飞帝王州[3]。
凤无琅玗[4]实，
何以赠远游？
徘徊相顾影，
泪下汉江流。

① 江夏：唐代县名，今武昌。
② 雪点翠云裘：借宋玉《讽赋》“翳承日之华，披翠云之裘”之义。
③ 帝王州：指唐代首都长安城。
④ 琅玗：这里指传说和神话中的仙树，其实似珠，作为凤凰的食物。

Seeing off a Friend off in Jiangxia City ①

With th' furgarment-like clouds the snowflakes fly,
I see off thee to leave Yellow Crane Tower.
The yellow crane ② flutters his wings on high
Westwards to th' Capital of the Empire.
Like phoenix, I've no Langgan fruits be fed, ③
I've nil to give thee for thy journey long;
Just have to linger 'long with my own shade,
Shedding my trears as th' Hanjiang ④ flows along.

---

① **Jiangxia City** the nowaday Wuchang, Hubei Province.

② **The yellow crane** a metaphor of his friend whom the poet sees off.

③ **Phoenix** here is a metaphor of an extraordinary person; **Langgan** a kind of divine tree in a Chinese tale, of which the pearl-like fruits can be fed phoenix. The whole line means that the poet cannot serve the government or society because he has no supporting condition as his friend does; and it also means he has no money to buy his friend a gift.

④ **Hanjiang** the Hanjiang River.

将进酒

君不见黄河之水天上来，
奔流到海不复回。
君不见高堂[①]明镜悲白发，
朝如青丝暮成雪。
人生得意须尽欢，
莫使金樽空对月。
天生我材必有用，
千金散尽还复来。
烹羊宰牛且为乐，
会须一饮三百杯。
岑夫子[②]，丹丘生[③]，
将进酒，杯莫停。

① 高堂：这里指富丽豪华的厅堂。
② 岑夫子：岑勋，李白一挚友。
③ 丹丘生：元丹丘，李白另一挚友。此诗即写诗人和岑勋做客元丹丘府上的情境。

Wine, Please!

Don't you see the Yellow River come from Heaven
And surges waves huge to the sea but never return?
Don't you see in th' Hall the Nobles look in the mirror,
And sigh their black hair in th' morn turned white at vesper?
You'd carouse and 'joy yourself while in your glory,
Do not, beneath the moon, keep your wine cup empty.
Our talents Heaven endowed will be called into full play,
E'en if sumless gold is all spent, surely regain it we may.
Let's butcher cattle and sheep for a feast merry and fine,
And each of us should drink three hundred cups of wine.
My intimate friends, Monsieur Cen and Monsieur Yuan[①],
Wine, please! You shouldn't let the cup be off your hand.

---

① **Cen**, i.e., Cen Xun; Dan, i.e., **Yuan Danqiu**. They both were the friends of the poet.

与君歌一曲，
请君为我倾耳听。
钟鼓馔玉①不足贵，
但愿长醉不复醒。
古来圣贤皆寂寞，
惟有饮者留其名。
陈王②昔时宴平乐③，
斗酒十千恣④欢谑⑤。
主人何为言少钱，
径须沽取对君酌。
五花马，千金裘，
呼儿将出换美酒，
与尔同销万古愁！

---

① 馔（zhuàn）玉：形容食物如玉一样精美。
② 陈王：指陈思王曹植。
③ 平乐：观名，在洛阳西门外，为汉代富豪显贵的娱乐场所。
④ 恣：纵情任意。
⑤ 谑（xuè）：戏。

I now would like to sing a song to you, my crony,
And wish you with a great attention to hear me.
Worth nothing is the feast with drum sound merrier
We'd drink and drink till be dead lushed and not sober.
The sages have ever been in oblivion through ages,
But those who's e'er steeped in drink left 'hind their names.
Once th' Prince Chen ① in Pingle host'd a feast in grand cheer,
They'd drunk thousand a cup of wine which is much dear.
I wouldn't plain my money is less If I were th' host,
And just buy wine to drink with you at any cost.
Even th' steed strong and fine, and th' coat dear and smart,
May be sold for buying sweet wine to drink
To drown the woe ever-haunting our heart!

---

① **The Prince Chen** i.e. Cao Zhi, the younger brother of Cao Pi, the emperor of Wei Kingdom during Three Kingdoms Period.

春夜洛城闻笛

谁家玉笛暗飞声，
散入春风满洛城。
此夜曲中闻折柳，
何人不起故园情。

Hearing Flute in Luoyang in a Spring Night

From whose abode the flute sounds a sweet song?
With spring breeze it fills Luoyang, the grand town.
Who ever not arouse the homesickness might
If hearing *Break Willow Twigs* in such a night?

洛阳陌

白玉[1]谁家郎，

回车渡天津[2]。

看花东陌[3]上，

惊动洛阳人。

① 白玉：喻美貌少年，形容其面如白玉。

② 天津桥：洛水上通往洛阳城的桥梁，也是当时洛阳一景。

③ 东陌：洛阳城东的大道，那里桃李成行，阳春时节，城中男女多去那里赏花。

On the Luoyang Road

Whose son, a lad with jade-like looks?
Back from th' Tianjin Bridge ① he's driving.
Along th' East Road ②, blooms he's 'holding,
Which draws Luoyang folks from all nooks.

---

① **Tianjin Bridge** i.e. Luoyang Bridge, a bridge across Luoshui River to Luoyang City.

② **The East Road** a grand road on the east of Luoyang City.

赠孟浩然

吾爱孟夫子，
风流天下闻。
红颜弃轩冕，
白首卧松云。
醉月频中圣，
迷花不事君。
高山安可仰，
徒此揖清芬。

To Meng Haoran

Thy honor, Master Meng, how much I admire thee!
Thou art widely renowned of the virtue fine.
In prime, thou waiv'st th' official voiture and leav'ry,
When aged, thou retreat'd in clouded woods of pine.
Enjoying drinking leisurely 'neath the moon bright,
Than serve the emperor thou wouldst rather flo'ers rear,
So 'dmired is thy character like a lofty height,
I pay my homage to thee with my heart sincere.

东鲁门[①]泛舟二首（其一）

日落沙明天倒开，
波摇石动水萦回。
轻舟泛月寻溪转，
疑是山阴雪后[②]来。

① 东鲁门：兖州城东。

② 山阴雪后：山阴，即今浙江绍兴。山阴雪后：据《世说新语·任诞》记载，东晋王徽家住山阴，一夜大雪纷飞，漫天皆白，忽然想起家住剡溪（在今浙江嵊州）的好友戴逵，便乘舟造访。经一夜行舟到达戴家门前，却不入门而返回。有人问其缘由，答曰："我本乘兴而来，兴尽而返，何必见戴？"

Boating beyond the East Gate of Yanahou (Two Poems, No. I)

The sun sets on th' shoal and mirror'd is sky,
Pebble shadows in th' ri'er flicker as swirls th' flow.
I'm boating 'long th' stream 'neath the moon on high,
As Wang ① left Shanyin for his friend's aft snow.

① **Wang** i.e. Wang Hui, a celeberity in East Jin Dynasty, who lived at Shanyin (nowday Shaoxing, Zhejiang Province). One night, snow fell, he was in heart and remembered his old friend, Dai Kui, an outstanding artist. He then left his home to call on Dai Kui who lived at Shanxi (nowaday Shengzhou, Zhejiang Province). When he arrived at the front of Dai's gate after a long journey in a whole night, he instantly returned rather than enter Dai's resident. He was asked why he didn't come in Dai's home to see him, he said: "I just come while in high spririts and I'm already satisfied with the journey. Why must I meet him?"

短歌行

白日何短短，
百年[①]苦易满。
苍穹浩茫茫，
万劫[②]太极[③]长。
麻姑[④]垂两鬓，
一半已成霜。
天公见玉女[⑤]，
大笑亿千场。
吾欲揽六龙，
回车挂扶桑。

---

① 百年：一生；终身。
② 万劫：犹万世，形容时间极长。佛经称世界从生成到毁灭的过程为一劫。“劫，世也。儒谓之世，道谓之尘，佛谓之劫。”
③ 太极：这里指天地未分以前的元气。
④ 麻姑：神话中仙女名。
⑤ 玉女：仙女。

Song of the Unabiding Life

How sooner a day elapses,
A whole life will soon finds its end.
The sky is so vast and boundless,
Th' universe might indefinite extend.
Magu's ① temples have become grey,
Turned white has half the hair of Her.
Th' Heaven Emperor ② and fairy ③
Pitch at pot ④, bursting myriad a laughter.

I'll halt six dragons that pull th' Carrier
Of th' Sun ⑤, and park it on th' Fusang ⑥.

---

① **Magu** a goddess in Chinese myth.

② **Heaven Emperor** the ruler of Heaven; the supreme ruler of the universe.

③ **Fairy** goodness in heaven.

④ **Pitch at pot** a game that the participants picth arrows into a necked pot. The winer, of course, laughes because of joy. "The Heaven Emperor and fairy//Pitch at pot, bursting myriad a laughter" means a long time has elapsed.

⑤ **Six dragons pull the Carrier of the Sun.** According to a Chinese myth, the sun's carriage is pulled by six dragons. The Carrier of the Sun, here referring to the Sun's carriage.

⑥ **Fusang** a name of ancient place (in Chinese myth), where Fusang Trees enormously grew.

北斗酌美酒，
劝龙各一觞。
富贵非所愿，
与人驻颜光。

Then spoon up wine with Big Dipper
To serve each dragon with a cup of wine. ①
Craving not for th' wealth and honor,
I'll stay th' flying time to keep young looks fine.

---

① **To serve a cup for each dragon**, to fed dragons with wine to let them rest even fall into sleep, no longer continue to pull the of the sun so that the flying time can halt.

送友人

青山横北郭，
白水[①]绕东城。
此地一为别，
孤蓬[②]万里征。
浮云游子意，
落日故人情。
挥手自兹去，
萧萧班马[③]鸣。

---

① 白水：清澈的水。

② 蓬：古书上说的一种植物，干枯后根株断开，遇风飞飘，也称“飞蓬”。这里用“孤蓬”喻指远行的朋友。

③ 班马：离群的马。

Seeing off a Friend

Around the east city runs th' river clear,
Green mountain lies on the north of the town.
I will bid a farewell to you from here,
Then you start your long trip like thistledown.
You'll wander as if a drifting cloud in skies,
But hate to leave as th' sun's loath to go down.
Even our horses breathe off loud cries
When you wave to depart from this town.

寄淮南[1]友人

红颜[2]悲旧国，
青岁[3]歇芳洲。
不待金门诏[4]，
空持宝剑游。
海云迷驿道，
江月隐乡楼。
复作淮南客，
因逢桂树留。

---

① 淮南：淮南道，治所位于扬州。
② 红颜：年轻人红润的脸色。这里代指年轻时期。亦可参见诗人的《赠孟浩然》。
③ 春岁：青春的年龄。这里指天宝七年春，与白毫子一起游历八公山。
④ 金门诏：金门，这里指朝廷。金门诏，即皇帝的诏书。

Staying in a Friend's in Huainan

In my bloom①, sighs o'er th' Capital I used to make,
As a youth, I now relax in a town full of th' flo'er.
Having not been summomèd by the Golden Gate②,
I, with my sharp sword, take so leisurely a tour.
The courier roads are lost 'mid clouds over th' brine,
The moon has fallen behind the country mansions.
Being a guest again in Huainan, a haunt fine,
I'm inclined to linger here because of fragrans.

---

① **Bloom** one's age of youth.

② **Golden Gate** a metaphor of the imperial court.

南阳送客

斗酒勿为薄[1]，
寸心贵不忘。
坐[2]惜故人去，
偏令游子伤。
离颜怨芳草，
春思结垂杨。
挥手再三别，
临岐空断肠。

---

① 薄：少。
② 坐：深。

A Farewell to a Guest in Nanyang

A hodful wine, carp not if not enow,
Our friendship e'er be kept in menmory.
I'm loath to part with you who's to leave now,
Which makes me lost into my heart gloomy.
My sad looks blame for the flowers that blow [①],
And trust'd on willow is my yearning heart.
Waving hand to bid a farewell to you,
I'm drowned in my broken heart when we part.

---

① **blow** (of flowers, blosoms) to bloom; to come into blooming.

游南阳清泠泉[①]

惜彼落日暮，
爱此寒泉清。
西辉逐流水，
荡漾游子情。
空歌望云月，
曲尽长松声。

① 清泠泉：位于南阳丰山下的自然景观。

Paying a Visit the Clear Fountain in Nanyang

I'm loath to hehold fade th' vesper view,
And enjoy th' lovely Cool Fountain's hue.
The setting sun's mirror'd in flow rippling
Which is much like my emontions surging.
I can't but sing loud while gazing th' moon fine,
Whereafter hear soughing are the woods of pine.

客中[①]行

兰陵[②]美酒郁金[③]香，
玉碗盛来琥珀光。
但使主人能醉客，
不知何处是他乡。

① 客中：指旅居他乡。
② 兰陵：原山东峄县，在今山东枣庄南。
③ 郁金：一种香草。

Being a Guest in the Alien Land

Shedding balm of curcuma is Lanling wine,
In the jade bowl, it flashes the amber shine.
When the host let me drink entirely down,
I can't help taking here as my hometown.

忆东山二首（其一）

不向东山[①]久，
蔷薇几度花？
白云还自散，
明月落谁家？

① 东山：又名谢安山，位于今浙江上虞市西南四十五里，晋太傅谢安隐居之地。

Yearning for the East Hill (Two Poems, No. I)

I've for long not been to th' East Hill ①,
Do th' roses there still bloom and fall?
Do clouds there drift far and wide still?
On whose abode will th' bright moon call? ②

---

① **East Hill** also called Xie Anshan, located in the southwest more than twenty kilometrs away from Shangyu County, Zhejiang Province.

② **On whose abode will th' bright moon call?** Here the bright moon may refer to a fair whom the poet admires.

相逢行

相逢红尘内，
高揖黄金鞭。
万户垂杨里，
君家阿那边。

Meeting by Chance

In th' downtown, I fancy meeting you,
What a gold-dighted whip you hold!
In such a huge quarter willows grow,
May you tell me where's your abode?

估客行

海客[①]乘天风，
将船[②]远行役[③]。
譬如云中鸟，
一去无踪迹。

① 海客：海上旅客，这里指出海做生意的商客。
② 将船：驾船。
③ 行役：有关旅行的事宜，这里指从事经商，出海做生意。

The Trader Out to the Sea

The trader sails his boat far cry,
By right of the wind 'neath vast sky
As if a bird amid cloud flies,
He soon fade away from my eyes.

蜀[1]道难

噫吁嚱[2]！
危乎高哉！
蜀道之难，难于上青天！

蚕丛及鱼凫[3]，
开国何茫然！
尔来四万八千岁，
不与秦塞通人烟。
西当太白有鸟道，
可以横绝峨眉巅。

---

① 蜀：古国名，位于四川一带。
② 噫吁嚱：惊叹声，表示惊讶。
③ 蚕丛及鱼凫：传说中古蜀国开国时期的两位国王的名字。

Hard is the Road to Shu State①

Oh! How steep and high
Is th' Road to Shu State!
Hard is the Road②, 'tis harder than to go up to the sky!

Since Cancong and Yufu③, th' two pioneers
Long, long ago inaugurat'd
The State④, passed have thousands of years,
But She's never in contact with Chin State⑤.
Only birds can westward fly over Taibai Height⑥
Up to the height of Mount Emei⑦ lofty.

---

① **Shu State** an ancient state. It became an administrative area under the reign of Tang Dynasty.

② **the Road** the above-mentioned the Road to Shu State.

③ **Cancong and Yufu** two ancient kings of Shu State which was inaugurated by them.

④ **the State** the above-mentioned Shu State.

⑤ **Chin State** a state during the Period of Warring States in ancienat China. It became the center of Tang Dynasty.

⑥ **Taibai Height** the crest of Taibai Mountain which is the highest mountain located in the regiom of Chin State, the hub of Tang Dynasty for which Taibai Mountain here substitutes. Chin is the ancient state and the first feudal dynasty in China.

⑦ **Mount Emei** the highest mountain in the region of ancient Shu State fot which Mount Emei here substitutes.

地崩山摧壮士死[①]，
然后天梯石栈方钩连。

上有六龙回日[②]之高标[③]，
下有冲波逆折之回川。
黄鹤之飞尚不得过，
猿猱欲度愁攀援。
青泥何盘盘[④]，
百步九折萦岩峦。
扪参历井仰胁息[⑤]，
以手抚膺坐[⑥]长叹。

① 地崩山摧壮士死：据《华阳国志·蜀志》：秦惠王欲征蜀国，知其王好色，便答应送其五美女。遂蜀王派五壮士接人。返途中至梓潼（今四川剑阁之南）时，见一大蛇入穴中，一壮士遂抓其尾，余四人相助，用力向外拖拽。霎时，山崩地裂，壮士和美女均被乱石覆压而死。大山分为五岭，入蜀之路遂通。

② 六龙回日：据《淮南子》注："日乘车，驾以六龙。羲和御之。日至此面而薄于虞渊，羲和至此而回六螭。"也即羲和驾驶着六龙之车（即太阳）至此处便迫近虞渊（传说中的日落处）。

③ 高标：指蜀山中可作一方标识的最高峰。

④ 青泥：青泥岭，位于今甘肃徽县南、陕西略阳县北。

⑤ 扪参历井仰胁息：历：经过。参（shēn）、井系古代天文学上的两星宿名。古人把天上的星宿分别指配于地上的州国，称为"分野"，以便通过观察天象来占卜地上所配州国的吉凶。参星为蜀之分野，井星为秦之分野。胁息，屏气不敢呼吸。

⑥ 膺（yīng）：胸；坐：徒，空。

Aft mountains crumbled, which had the trail-blazing warriors died.
Blazed were th' trails heav'n-ladder-like and paths rocky-and-risky.

Above, blocking the Helios' carriage① is the crest high,
Below, surging are the winding and waving rivers.
Across them even the yellow cranes can't fly,
And an apes scares when the mountain he clambers.
The tortuous trail on the Green Mudy Ridge② high,
Winds around the ranges of cragged mountain.
Holding breath and looking up, I nearly touch the Stars③ in sky,
Pressing chest with hands' cause of fear, I make a deep sigh in vain.

---

① **Helios' carriage** i.e. the Sun's carriage. See note ⑤ of *A Song of the Unabiding Life*.

② **Green Mudy Ridge** a mountain straddles Shaanxi and Gansu.

③ **the Stars** here referring to the Star of Shen, which represents the scope of Shu State, and the Star of Jing, which represent the scope of Qin State.

问君西游何时还？
畏途巉岩不可攀。
但见悲鸟号古木，
雄飞雌从绕林间。
又闻子规啼夜月，
愁空山。
蜀道之难，难于上青天，
使人听此凋朱颜。

连峰去天不盈尺，
枯松倒挂倚绝壁。
飞湍瀑流争喧豗，
砯崖[①]转石万壑雷。
其险也若此，
嗟尔远道之人胡为乎来哉！

① 砯（pīng）崖：水撞石之声。

When wilt thou return from the tour to west, may I ask thee?
How wilt thou trek through such sheer and perilous trails
Where only birds in the ancient woods you can see?
The females chase after the ahead-flying males
In the moonlit night, cuckoos constant shrill
Over th' gaunt mountains, making one sorrow and thrill.
Hard is the Road, 'tis harder than to go up to the sky!
One will turn pale when he hears what I tell.

The peak is just no more than a foot off the sky,
With their heads down, the ancient pines grow on the cliffs sheer.
Torrant and turbulence in roaring vie
As billows beat the scars and roars thousand a thunder.
How dangerous such haunts are!
Why dost thou from afar come hither?

剑阁峥嵘而崔嵬[①]，

一夫当关，

万人莫开。

所守或匪亲，

化为狼与豺。

朝避猛虎，

夕避长蛇，

磨牙吮血，

杀人如麻。

锦城[②]虽云乐，

不如早还家。

蜀道之难，难于上青天，

侧身西望长咨嗟[③]！

---

① 剑阁：又名剑门关，位于在四川剑阁县北，是大剑山和小剑山之间的一条栈道，长约三十余里。峥嵘、崔嵬（wéi）：均为形容山势高大巍峨的样子。

② 锦城：锦官城，即今四川省成都市。

③ 长咨（zī）嗟：长叹。咨嗟，叹息。

The Sword Pass is so steep a scar[①] !
E'en one man it guards,
Thousands can't it pass.
If th' guards're disloyal, they might become traitors
To rise in revolt as foes like cruel wolves and pards.
At morn, one must escape from tigers,
At dusk, he has to avoid the serpents
As vampire with sharp teeth does blood drain,
The two kinds of beasts devour a man as if engulf a fly.
Although Jinguan is the best haunt to make merry,
I would rather go home soon.
Hard is the Road, 'tis harder than to go up to the sky!
I turn round and gaze at the west with so deep a sigh!

① **scar** a cliff.

长门怨（其二）

桂殿[①]长愁不记春[②]，
黄金四屋[③]起秋尘。
夜悬明镜[④]青天上，
独照长门宫里人。

① 桂殿：指长门殿。
② 不记春：不知春天已到来，引申为不知现为何年何月。
③ 四屋：四壁。
④ 夜悬明镜：指明月。

Resentment from the Outcasts' Palace (Two Poems, No. II)

She know not what year it is 'cause of life in drear,
All the walls of the palace are veiled with dusts.
The bright moon like a mirror hangs in the sky clear,
She is alone shining over the palace's outcasts.

塞下曲六首（其一）

五月天山[①]雪，
无花只有寒。
笛中闻折柳[②]，
春色未曾看。
晓战随金鼓[③]，
宵眠抱玉鞍。
愿将腰下剑，
直为斩楼兰[④]。

① 天山：此诗中的天山指祁连山，而非横跨中国、哈萨克斯坦、吉尔吉斯斯坦和乌兹别克斯坦四国的天山。匈奴呼天为“祁连”，故祁连山即为天山。

② 折柳：古乐曲《折杨柳》。

③ 金鼓：金锣。古代打仗进攻是击鼓，退兵时鸣金（锣）。

④ 楼兰：汉代西域少数民族政权，屡犯汉朝边塞。

Song of Northwest Frontier (Six Poems, No. I)

In summer Tianshan[①] is clad with snows still,
There are no flowers in blooming but chill.
Though I hear *Break Willow Twigs*, a tune of fluting,
Yet I've still not beheld the hue of spring.
In th' day, as gongs and drums sound, solders fight,
And just sleep on the saddle during th' night.
They're so eager to kill the Tartar pards[②],
With their waist-holding incisive swords.

---

① **Tianshan** here referring to Qilian Mountain.

② **Tartar pards** a metaphor for brutal Tartar foes.

送友人入蜀

见说蚕丛路[①]，
崎岖不易行。
山从人面起[②]，
云傍马头生[③]。
芳树笼秦栈[④]，
春流[⑤]绕蜀城。
升沉应已定，
不必问君平[⑥]。

① 蚕丛：蜀国的开国君王。蚕丛路：代称入蜀的道路。
② 山从人面起：人在栈道上走时，紧靠峭壁，山崖好像从人的脸侧突兀而起。
③ 云傍马头生：云气依傍着马头而上升翻腾。
④ 秦栈：由秦（今陕西省）入蜀的栈道。
⑤ 春流：春江水涨，江水奔流。
⑥ 君平：西汉的严遵，字君平，隐居不仕，曾在成都以占卜为生。

Seeing off a Friend for Shu State

You must have heard how hard and craggy
Is the road to Shu State Cancong ① ploughed.
E'en your face will touch th' crags when you trudgé,
Over the head of your horse floats the cloud.
By lushy trees the plank-trail all are twined,
Runs around Jinguan City th' spring river.
Our fate, either rise or fall, is destined,
Why need we ask Yan Zun ②, a diviner?

---

① **Cancong** see note ③ of *Hard is the Road to the Shu State* in this book.

② **Yan Zun** a diviner, also named Yan Junping, in Western Han Dynsaty, who lived on divining.

清平调三首（一）

云想衣裳花想容，
春风拂槛露华浓。
若非群玉山头见，
会向瑶台月下逢。

Ode to Ranee Yang (Three Poems, No. I)

Eager to be her ① 'ttire is th' cloud and her looks th' flower,
Standing on th' rail, caressed by spring breeze is the fair ②.
Such a beauty merely seen on the Jades Hill' ③ height,
Or met in the Lake of Jasper ④ 'neath the moon bright.

---

① **her** the fair mentioned in the following line of this poem.

② **the fair** here referring to Yang Yuhuan, the concubine of the Xuanzong Emperor (Li Longji) in Tang Dynasty.

③ **Jades Hill** a fairy hill in Chinese myth.

④ **Lake of Jasper** also a fairy land where fairies dwell.

杜陵绝句

南登杜陵[①]上，
北望五陵[②]间。
秋水明落日，
流光灭远山。

① 杜陵：位于今陕西省西安市东南，为西汉宣帝刘询的陵墓，位于渭水南岸。

② 五陵：唐颜师古《汉书》注："五陵，谓长陵、安陵、阳陵、茂陵、平陵。"汉高祖葬长陵，惠帝葬安陵，景帝葬阳陵，武帝葬茂陵，昭帝葬平陵，均在渭水北岸，今陕西省咸阳市附近。后人用五陵多指豪门贵族聚居之地或指豪门贵族。

A Quatrain on Duling Tomb ①

I now ascend Duling Tomb on th' south bank, ②
Gazing afar Five Tombs ③ on the north bank. ④
Th' setting sun's mirror'd in th' autumn river,
The sun beams die 'way 'hind th' mountains yonder.

---

① **Duling Tomb** the Mausoleum of Emperor Xuan (Liu Xun) of West Han Dynasty, located on the south bank of Weishui River.

② **the south bank** referring to the south bank of Weishui River.

③ **Five Tombs** referring to a cluster of tombs of the emperors of West Han Dynasty, including Liu Bang, Liu Ying, Liu Qi, Liu Che and Liu Fuling.

④ **the north bank** referring to the north bank of Weishui River.

灞陵行送别

送君灞陵亭①，
灞水②流浩浩。
上有无花之古树，
下有伤心之春草。
我向秦人问路岐，
云是王粲③南登之古道。
古道连绵走西京，
紫阙落日浮云生。
正当今夕断肠处，
骊歌④愁绝不忍听。

① 灞陵亭：古亭名，在长安东灞水之滨，为古人饯别之地。
② 灞水：源出陕西蓝田县东，北流入渭水。浩浩：形容水势广大的样子。
③ 王粲：东汉末文学家。
④ 骊歌：离别之歌。

Seeing off a Friend at Baling Bower

I see you off from the Baling Bower,
Fiercely surging is the Bashui River.
Above, the old trees are devoid of bloom,
Below, the spring grass is laden with gloom.
I ask a native which is your right way:
"Take th' southward one, which Wang[①] once chose, you may."
The long ancient road stretches to the Capital,
Clouds rise while 'hind th' Palace th' sun's to fall.
At th' haunt where we're lost in bro'en-heart this e'ening,
How can we endure hearing *Song of Parting*?

---

① **Wang** referring to Wang Can, a famous writer in the Eastern Han Dynasty.

把酒问月

青天有月来几时？
我今停杯一问之。
人攀明月不可得，
月行却与人相随。
皎如飞镜临丹阙①，
绿烟②灭尽清辉发。
但见宵从海上来，
宁知③晓向云间没？
白兔捣药秋复春④，
嫦娥⑤孤栖与谁邻？

---

① 丹阙：朱红色的宫殿。
② 绿烟：指遮蔽月光的浓重的云雾。
③ 宁知：怎知。
④ 白兔捣药秋复春：神话传说月仙兔成年为嫦娥捣仙药。西晋傅玄《拟天问》："月中何有，白兔捣药。"
⑤ 嫦娥：一作"姮娥"，神话中的月宫中的女神。传说她原是后羿的妻子，偷吃了后羿的仙药成仙，奔入月宫。见《淮南子·览冥训》。

Asking About the Moon While Drinking

When will the moon beneath the azure rise?
I put down the wine cup to ask the skies.
Never can man reach to the moon bright,
But she e'er follows us where be we might.
Like a mirror over palace in red①,
She sheds her sheen after haze has fled.
We see she rises on the sea at night,
But know not in the morn where she'll hide.
The Jade Hare② makes exlixir all the year
For Chang'e③ who's still lone with no partner.

---

① **Palace in red** the palaces in ancient China were generally painted in red color.

② **The Jade Hare** a fairy animal in the Moon Palace who pounds elixir for Chang'e year after year.

③ **Chang'e** a fairy female figure in Chinese myth, the wife of Yi who was the sixth emperor of Xia Dynasty. It was said that Chang'e had flown into the Moon Palace because of covertly taking the forbidden elixir.

今人不见古时月，
今月曾经照古人。
古人今人若流水，
共看明月皆如此。
唯愿当歌对酒时，
月光长照金樽里。

The moon in ancient we've never beheld,
But th' moon tonight once shone over the eld.
We and th' eld are like the flow of river,
Both share the same bright moon forever.
I wish moonlight be cast into my cup of wine
When I drink and sing towards the moon in shine.

月下独酌四首（其一）

花间一壶酒，
独酌无相亲[①]。
举杯邀明月，
对影成三人[②]。
月既不解[③]饮，
影徒[④]随我身。
暂伴月将[⑤]影，
行乐须及春[⑥]。
我歌月徘徊，
我舞影零乱。

---

① 无相亲：没有亲人（陪伴）。
② 对影成三人：我杯邀请明月，明月和我以及我的影子三人一起共饮。一说月下人影、酒中人影和我为三人共饮。
③ 不解：不懂；不理解。
④ 徒：只；但。
⑤ 将：和，与，共。
⑥ 及春：趁着春光明媚之时。

Drinking Alone beneath the Moon (Four Poems, No. I)

Bringing a flagon of wine amid flowers,
I drink alone, without any partners.
Raising my cup to invite th' moon on high
As if three souls, the moon, my shade and I
Drink 'gether, but not know drinking does She,
And my shade all the time closely she follows me.
I'm being, for a while, with th' moon and my shade,
To make merry in time ere th' spring's to fade.
The moon is lingering while I'm singing,
And my shade is waggling while I'm dancing.

醒时同交欢[①]，
醉后各分散。
永结无情游[②]，
相期邈云汉[③]。

① 同交欢：一起欢乐。
② 无情游：月、影无知觉，不懂感情，李白与之结交，故称“无情游”。
③ 相期邈云汉：约定在天上相见。相期，相约会。邈，遥远。云汉，即银河。这里指遥远的天际。

When I sober, we three gaily'gether play,
Aft being drunk, we each go one's own way.
I wish we three could play 'gether forever,
And would meet again in the heaven higher.

行路难三首（其一）

金樽清酒斗十千，
玉盘珍羞直万钱[①]。
停杯投箸不能食，
拔剑四顾心茫然。
欲渡黄河冰塞川，
将登太行雪满山。
闲来垂钓碧溪上，
忽复乘舟梦日边。
行路难！行路难！
多歧路，今安在？
长风破浪会有时[②]，
直挂云帆[③]济沧海。

① 珍羞：珍贵的菜肴。羞，同“馐”，美味的食物。直：通“值”。

② 长风破浪会有时：比喻总有实现理想的时候。与诗人在《将进酒》中的“天生我材必有用”的豪言相一致。长风破浪，比喻实现政治理想。《宋书·宗悫传》载：宗悫少年时叔父宗炳问他的志向，答曰：“愿乘长风破万里浪。”

③ 云帆：高高的船帆。船在海里航行，因天水相连，船帆好像出没在云雾之中。

Hard Is the Way (Three Poems, No. I)

In golden cup, worthy of thousand golds is sweet wine,
In jade dish, even more precious are th' regales fine.
But I have no appetite and put th' chopstics aside,
A sword in hand, I, at loss, look at all a side.
I want to cross th' Yellow River, but 'tis frozen,
And try to climb Taihang, 'tis all snow-laden.
At leisure, I come fishing on so clear a stream
As if I sail my boat towards th' sun in a dream.
Hard is the road, hard is the way,
There're many a crossroad, which is the right way?
The time when rises a tide with east wind will be ①,
I will then set my sail to surf the surging sea ②.

---

① **The time when rises a tide with east wind will be** a tide: here referring to a high tide. It means the favorable or key time to do sth, (especially with the east wind). It is a metaphor for"a chance", as used in Shakespearean droma *Julius Caesar*:"There is a tide in the affairs of men which, taken at the flood (*the high tide*), leads on to fortune." The east wind: the favorale wind for a voyage, etc., even for a war as accounted in the novel of *Three Kingdoms*. So both the east wind and the high tide are symbolize a chance in the life of man.

② **to surf the surging sea** a metaphorical expression for "to serve the society", of course, through serving the court in that time during which the poet lived.

鲁郡[①]东石门送杜二甫

醉别复几日，
登临遍池台[②]
何时石门路，
重有金樽开[③]。
秋波落泗水[④]，
海色明徂徕[⑤]。
飞蓬各自远，
且尽手中杯。

---

① 鲁郡：唐代置，治所位于兖州，辖十县。
② 池台：池苑楼台。
③ 金樽开：开始举杯饮酒。
④ 泗水：水名，在山东省东部。
⑤ 徂（cú）徕（lái）：山名，位于今山东泰安市东南。

Farewell to Du Fu at Stone Gate Hill on the East of Yanzhou

We'd carouse, for we'll part in couple a day,
We've visit'd every lake and bower.
When meet again at the Stone Gate we may,
Rising the gold cup to drink together?
On th' Sishui River the ripples arise,
Culai Hill's mirrored on the sea flow.
We'll go far apart as thistledown flies,
So we should drink enough cups of wine now.

沙丘城[1]下寄杜甫

我来竟何事，
高卧沙丘城。
城边有古树，
日夕连秋声。
鲁酒不可醉，
齐歌空复情。
思君若汶水，
浩荡寄南征。

① 沙丘城：指现在的兖州城，也曾称瑕丘城。

To Du Fu from Sandhill Town ①

For what I come to Sandhill Town
Where I stay at ease all day long?
The ancient trees grow by th' townside,
Autumn sound is heard day and night.
I'm neither drunk by drinking th' local wine,
Nor toutched by the native song fine,
But miss you much as if th' Wenshui Ri'er
Swift surges southwards forever.

---

① **Sandhill Town** nowaday Yanzhou City, Shandong Province..

登金陵[1]凤凰台[2]

凤凰台上凤凰游，
凤去台空江自流。
吴宫[3]花草埋幽径，
晋代衣冠[4]成古丘[5]。
三山[6]半落青天外，
二水中分白鹭洲[7]。
总为浮云能蔽日[8]，
长安[9]不见使人愁！

---

① 金陵：古代南京之别称。
② 凤凰台：古塔台，位于金陵凤凰山。
③ 吴宫：三国时期东吴的宫殿。东吴曾建都金陵。
④ 晋代衣冠：晋代皇宫贵族奢华的衣饰。东晋曾建都金陵。
⑤ 古丘：坟墓。
⑥ 三山：山名。《景定建康志》记载："其山积石森郁，滨于大江，三峰并列，南北相连，故号三山。"
⑦ 白鹭洲：古代长江中的沙洲，洲上多集白鹭，故名。
⑧ 浮云蔽日：比喻谗臣当道，障蔽贤良。浮云：比喻奸邪小人。陆贾《新语·慎微篇》："邪臣之蔽贤，犹浮云之障日月也。"日：双关，同时指代帝王。
⑨ 长安：这里用京城借代朝廷和皇帝。

Ascending the Phoenix Stage ① in Jinling ②

On Phoenix Stage the phoenixes had been for play,
The birds had flown away but the river still waves.
Wu Palace ③ ruins are covered with th' grass by a sideway,
And the magnates of Jin ④ had been buried in graves.
Three Hills loom about in distance beyond skyline,
The Egret Isle ⑤ in the ri'er cleaves th' flow apart.
The floating dark clouds ever blind the sunshine ⑥,
Chang'an ⑦ is out of sight, but in my sorrow heart.

---

① **Phoenix Stage** a stage or tower located in Jinling.

② **Jinling** an ancient name of Nanjing City.

③ **Wu Palace** the imperial palace of Wu State during Three Kingdoms Period.

④ **the magnates of Jin** the luxury clothes and ornaments of the nobles of Jin Dynasty.

⑤ **The Egret Isle** an ancient sand isle in the Yangtze River, now died out.

⑥ **The floating dark clouds always blind the sunshine.** It is a pun implying those treacherous courtiers who push out the worthy ones and deceive the emperor.

⑦ **Chang'an** here is a substitution for the court or emperor.

酬崔侍御[①]

严陵[②]不从万乘[③]游，
归卧空山钓碧流[④]。
自是客星[⑤]辞帝座，
元非[⑥]太白醉扬州。

① 崔侍御：崔成富甫，李白之友，曾任摄监察御史（故李白称其为崔侍御），后因事被贬职到湘阴（今属湖南）。曾作有《赠李十二》诗给李白。此为李白答诗。

② 严陵：严子陵，名光，东汉人。少曾与刘秀同游学。刘秀即帝位后，严光变更姓名隐遁。刘秀遣人觅访，征授谏议大夫，不受，退隐于富春山。

③ 万乘：本义为皇帝出行的车队，这里代指皇帝。

④ 碧流：指富春江，严子陵隐居于富春江畔。

⑤ 客星：指严子陵。据《后汉书。严光传》：严子陵与光武帝共卧，足加与帝腹。太史奏：客星犯御座甚急。

⑥ 元非：原非。

Reply to Imperial Censor Cui ①

Yan Guang ② refused to be th' courtier of th' emperor,
He's back to th' green hill to fish in th' Fuchun River ③.
I also take leave from th' Sovran to be a recluse,
But not Taibai who's in Yangzhou as a winebibber.

---

① **Imperal Censor Cui** Cui Chengfu, an imperial censor.

② **Yan Guang** also named Yan Ziling. He was once a friend of Liu Xiu, the Emperor of Eastern Han Dynasty at his youth years before Liu Xiu was crowned. He refused to accept the high place, offered by Liu after being crowned, rather to be a hermit, doing farming and fishing, at his native place by the Fuchun River.

③ **Fuchun River** the native place of Yan Ziling, where he retreated to be as a hermit.

送陆判官[1]往琵琶峡[2]

水国[3]秋风夜，
殊非[4]远别时。
长安如梦里，
何日是归期。

---

① 陆判官：生平不详。判官，官名，唐时节度使等的下属官吏。
② 琵琶峡：在巫山，形同琵琶，故名。
③ 水国：水乡。
④ 殊非：绝非。

Seeing off the Prefect Assistant Lu to Pipa Gorge

'Tis not the time to leave th' town with ri'erflows
At such a night that th' autumn wind fierce blows.
Chang'an's best for career as we ro'ers dream,
At what date will you come back to this realm?

闻王昌龄左迁龙标遥有此寄

杨花落尽子规[①]啼，
闻道龙标[②]过五溪[③]。
我寄愁心与明月，
随风直到夜郎[④]西。

① 子规：杜鹃鸟。
② 龙标：王昌龄被贬去任职的县名，古人常用官职或任官之地的州县名来称呼一个人。
③ 五溪：一般指雄溪、满溪、潕溪、酉溪、辰溪的总称。
④ 夜郎：一般指夜郎国（古国），这是我国在西南地区由少数民族的先民建立的第一个国家政权。唐代在今贵州桐子和湖南沅陵等地设过夜郎县。这里指湖南的夜郎。李白当时在东南的苏州，所以说“随风直到夜郎西”。

From Afar to Wang Changling Who's Relegated to Longbiao County

At th' season willows shed catkins up and cuckoos cry,
I heard you'll fare for Longbiao and the Five Streams pass by.
I trust it on th' Moon that I'm concern'd about your fate,
Riding wind, it'll go with you to th' west of Yelang State. ①

① **Yelang State** an ancient state, located in the southwest of China, to the west of which Wang Changling was relegated.

宣州谢朓楼饯别校书叔云

弃我去者，
昨日之日不可留；
乱我心者，
今日之日多烦忧。
长风万里送秋雁，
对此可以酣高楼。
蓬莱文章建安骨，
中间小谢又清发。

At a Foy to Li Yun ① in the North Tower ②

What has deserted me and then gone away
Is th' date of yester that'll never stay.
What makes my state of mind destroy'd
Is nothing but today's annoy
With high winds the autumn swans afar fly,
At such a moment we'd swig in th' Tower high.
Essays of Penglai ③ bear Jian' an Style's Vigor, ④
Poems of mine carry on Junior Xie' s color. ⑤

---

① **Li Yun** with an alias Li Hua, Uncle of Li Bai, an outstanding essayist and an Official Collator in Tang Dynasty.

② **North Tower** an alias of Xie Tiao Tower or Tower of Master Xie, which was built by Xie Tiao who then took the office of the Prefect of Xuanzhou.

③ **Essays of Penglai** a metaphor substituting for the essays of Li Yun who was an Official Collator in Tang Dynasty. Penglai, the substitution for Central Secretariat which Li Yun served. Here Essays of Penglai is a metaphor for the essays of Li Yun.

④ **Jian'an's Style Vigor** the style of writing, characterized by being vigorous, profound, manificent and miserable, developed by the poets and essayists of whom Cao Cao, Cao Pi and Cao Zhi as well as Seven Scholars (Kong Rong, Chen Lin, Wang Can, Xu Gan, Ruan Yu, Ying Yang and Liu Zhen) were the representative figures during Jian'an Period under the Reign of Emperor Xian (196-220), Western Han Dynasty(202BC–8 AD).

⑤ **Junior Xie's color** the style of Xie Tiao's poetry style, characterized by freshness and comeliness. Xie Tiao (464-499) was regarded as Junior Xie, the eponym of Xie Lingyun(385-433) who was called Senior Xie,corresponding to Xie Tiao, by the later generations .

俱怀逸兴壮思飞，
欲上青天揽明月。
抽刀断水水更流，
举杯消愁愁更愁。
人生在世不称意，
明朝散发弄扁舟。

With delight, we make our ideal fly
Upto the sky where to pick the moon we try.
The river's even surges faster when I sabre its flow,
While 'tis e'en graver when I drown it in wine my woe.
Now that in this world we cannot make our own way,
Why not we, with rufled hair, sail a boat off[①] next day?

---

① **sail a boat far off** a metaphor for seeking to live in seclusion. It is inaugurated forth from the following historical story. In the end of Spring and Autumn Period (770-476BC), Fan Li (536 BC-448 BC), the Adviser to Goujian (c. 520-465 BC), the King of Yue State, went away, with unkempt hair, from Goujian by a boat, retreating to live in seclusion after Guojian annihilated Wu State reigned by the King Fuchai (c. 528-473 BC).

谢公亭

谢公[①]离别处[②]，
风景每生愁。
客散青天月，
山空碧水流。
池花春映日，
窗竹夜鸣秋。
今古一相接，
长歌怀旧游。

① 谢公：谢朓（464—499），字玄晖，斋号高斋，陈郡阳夏县（今河南省太康县）人，南齐诗人。

② 离别处：指谢朓与范云在此分别。范云（451—503），字彦龙，南乡郡舞阴县（今河南省泌阳县）人。南朝梁时期宰相、著名政治家、文学家、诗人。

Bower of Master Xie

Master Xie ① once parted with Master Fan ② here,
I'm lost in sorrow when seeing this bower.
They'd parted whereas the moon still shines clear,
The lone hill stands and flows the green river.
Flowers in th' pool smile towards th' sun in spring,
At autumn nights rustle th'bamboos outside window.
A close communion with th' elds ③ I'm feeling,
Singing a song, I recall their tour with sorrow.

---

① **Master Xie** Xie Tiao, an outstanding poet of Qi Dynasty during Southern Dynasties.

② **Master Fan** Fan Yun (451-503) ,also named Fan Yanlong, a famous politician, litereur and poet of Liang Dynasty during South Dynasties.

③ **The elds** here referring to Master Xie and Master Fan.

独坐敬亭山

众鸟高飞尽，
孤云独去闲。
相看两不厌。
只有敬亭山。

Sitting Alone in the Mount Jingting

All birds have flew away on high,
A cloud leisurely floats in sky.
Only am I with Jingtinig hither,
We are not tired of each ather.

听蜀僧睿[1]弹琴

蜀僧抱绿绮[2]，
西下峨眉峰。
为我一挥手，
如听万壑松。
客心洗流水，
馀响入霜钟[3]。
不觉碧山暮，
秋云暗几重。

---

① 蜀僧睿：名为睿的一名蜀僧。
② 绿绮：琴名。
③ 霜钟：晚秋的钟声。

Hearing Lute Playing by Monk Rui Who's from Shu State

Holding a dear lute in hands, Monk Rui of Shu State
Descends from the westside of the Emei Mountain.
He plucks the strings to play a tune for my sake,
I 'joy it as if hearing winds sough in woods of pine;
As if cleaning up my mind is th' mountain stream flows;
The echoing sound as though an autumn bell flies high.
I've not scent'd out the blue hill is veiled in dusk hues,
Getting thick and dark are the autumn clouds in sky.

秋登宣城[1]谢朓北楼[2]

江城[3]如画里，
山[4]晚望晴空。
两水夹明镜[5]，
双桥[6]落彩虹[7]。
人烟寒橘柚，
秋色老梧桐。
谁念北楼上，
临风怀谢公？

---

① 宣城：唐宣州，天宝元年（742 年）改为宣城郡，今属安徽省。

② 谢朓北楼：谢朓楼，又名谢公楼，唐代改名叠嶂楼，为南朝齐诗人谢朓任宣城太守时所建，故址在陵阳山顶，是宣城的登览胜地。

③ 江城：泛指水边的城，这里指宣城。唐代江南地区，无论大小水都称之为江城。

④ 山：指位于宣城的陵阳山。

⑤ 两水夹明镜：两水，指宛溪、句溪。宛溪上有凤凰桥，句溪上有济川桥。明镜，指拱桥桥洞和它在水中的倒影合成的圆形，像明亮的镜子一样。

⑥ 双桥：指横跨溪水的上、下两桥。上桥即凤凰桥，在城的东南泰和门外；下桥即济川桥，在城东阳德门外，均为隋文帝开皇年间（581—600）的水上建筑。

⑦ 彩虹：这里指水中的桥影。

Ascending the North Tower[①] at Xuancheng[②] in Autumn

The ri'erside city seems from a painting to rise,
At even on the Hill[③] I gaze at the clear skies.
A mirror emerges betwixt the two rivers[④],
Like rainbows the two bridges[⑤] alights on waters.
Made oranges chilly has the smoke of chimneys,
The autumn hue has withered the Phoenix trees.
Who can understand me to ascend the North Tower
In such a chilly wind to recall Xie, th' Great Master?

---

① **North Tower** an alias of Xie Tiao Tower or Tower of Master Xie at Xuancheng which was built by Xie Tiao who then took the office of the Prefect of Xuanzhou (Xuancheng).

② **Xuancheng** also called Xuanzhou, the seat of Xuanzhou Prefecture, located in nowaday Anhui Province.

③ **The Hill** referring to Lingyang Hill.

④ **The two rivers** referring to Wanxi Stream and Juxi Stream.

⑤ **Two bridges** referring to the Phoenix Bridge and Jichuan Bridge over the two rivers, Wanxi Stream and Juxi Stream, respectively.

秋浦歌十七首（其十五）

白发三千丈，
缘愁似个长。
不知明镜里，
何处得秋霜？

Songs of Qiupu River (Seventeen Poems, No. XV)

I wear white hair with thousand feet,
’Tis brought forth from my sorrow great.
I wonder how come has frost cold
In th’ mirror ’to which I behold?

宿清溪[①]主人

夜到清溪宿，
主人碧岩里。
檐楹挂星斗[②]，
枕席响风水[③]。
月落西山时，
啾啾夜猿起。

① 清溪：源出今安徽池州市南九华山，北流经池州市城东折西北入长江。

② 檐楹挂星斗：形容住宅所处地势的高。檐（yán），屋顶伸出的边沿。楹（yíng）：堂前的柱子，也指屋内天井四周的柱子。

③ 枕席响风水：夜间躺在床上听到外面瑟瑟风声和潺潺流水声。

Staying a Night at the Host's of the Clear Stream①

I come to the Clear Stream to stay a night,
The host lives on the Blue Rock's hillside.
Stars hang on th' house's eaves and front pillars,
Lying in bed, I hear winds whistle and stream bickers.
The nocturnal apes are ceaseless screaming
While behind the west hill th' moon is setting.

---

① **The Clear Stream** a river runs in Chizhou, Anhui Province.

清溪行

清溪清我心，
水色异诸水。
借问新安江，
见底何如此？
人行明镜中，
鸟度屏风里。
向晚猩猩啼，
空悲远游子。

Song of the Clear Stream

The Clear Stream does make my heart clear,
'Tis so distinctive from many a ri'er.
I'd like to ask Xin'an Ri'er: "Where canst thou
Find such a stream with the water see-through?"
On which boats sail as if racing in th' mirror,
Birds fly o'er it as if 'twixt screens hover.
Monkeys ceaseless scream when comes the even,
Which makes me sorrow, a rover alien.

赠汪伦

李白乘舟将欲行，
忽闻岸上踏歌声。
桃花潭[1]水深千尺，
不及汪伦送我情。

① 桃花潭：在今安徽泾县西南。

To Wang Lun

Boarding my boat, I'm 'bout to fare for my tour,
Amain hear you sing an adieu song on th' shore.
The Peach Bloom Pool ① is a thousand feet deep,
But it can't come up to your deep friendship.

① **Peach Blossom Pool** a lake located in the southwest of nowaday Tingxian County, Anhui Province.

从军行

百战沙场碎铁衣，
城南已合数重围。
突营射杀呼延将，
独领残兵千骑归。

Song of Army[①] (Two Poems, No. II)

His armor has been worn out aft many a bout;
Though besieged ring upon ring on th' south of city,
He killed th' head of Tartar troops and broke out,
Returning in th' end with his remnant cavalry.

---

① This poem describes a gallant general.

拟古十二首（其九）

生者为过客，
死者为归人。
天地一逆旅，
同悲万古尘。
月兔空捣药，
扶桑[1]已成薪。
白骨寂无言，
青松岂知春。
前后更叹息，
浮荣安足珍？

① 扶桑：古代神话传说中的地名。据《梁书·诸夷传·扶桑国》："扶桑在大汉国东二万余里，其土多扶桑树，故名。"

Poems in Ancient Style (Twelve Poems, No. IX)
——Life and Fame

One who's alive is a passenger-by,
One who's dead a rover returning home.
And th' world is just a post-house beneath sky,
'Tis pity that all will 'to dust become.
Chang'e is ① lone though th' Hare ② makes her elixir,
Fusang ③ ' will turn 'to firewood to fuel flaming .
How can the white bones of the dead utter?
And th' evergreen pines feel not th' warmth of spring.
You'll sigh if you make a survey through ages,
'Tis just a vanity for one's prestiges.

---

① **Chang'e** a fairy female figure in Chinese myth, the wife of Yi who was the sixth emperor of Xia Dynasty. It was said that Chang'e had flown into the Moon Palace because of covertly taking the forbidden elixir.

② **the Hare** also called Jade Hare, a fairy animal in the Moon Palace who pounds elixir for Chang'e.

③ **Fusang** a name of ancient place (in Chinese legend), where Fusang Trees enormously grew.

永王东巡歌（十一首，其四）

龙盘虎踞帝王州，
帝子金陵访故丘。
春风试暖昭阳殿，
明月还过鳷鹊楼。

An Eastwards Inspectation Tour of Prince Yong (Eleven Poems, No. IV)

A royal city once ta'en by Dragons and Tighers ①
Is Jinling on which Prince Yong now makes a tour.
Zhaoyang Palace is caressed by spring breeze tender,
The beaming moon shines over the Megpie Tower.

---

① **Dragons and Tigers** here is a metaphor for the nobles and big wings.

与史郎中钦听黄鹤楼上吹笛

一为迁客去长沙，
西望长安不见家。
黄鹤楼中吹玉笛，
江城五月落梅花。

Hearing Flute with Director Shi Qin[①] at Yellow Crane Tower

I'm relegated to Changsha and will bear a blight,
Looking afar at Chang'an, my home's out of sight.
Sounds of flute fly out from the Yellow Crane Tower,
Wintersweets Fall in th' River[②] City in mid-summer.

---

① **Shi Qin** a friend of Li Bai.

② **the River City** here referring to Wuchang.

早发白帝城

朝辞白帝彩云间，
千里江陵[①]一日还。
两岸猿声啼不住，
轻舟已过万重山。

① 江陵：位于湖北省，今置江陵县。盛弘之《荆州记》："朝发白帝，暮宿江陵，凡一千二百余里，虽飞云速鸟，不能过也。"《水经注》："三峡七百里中，两岸连山略无缺处，常有高猿长啸。"

Leaving Baidi City at Dawn

Leaving Baidi City ① at dawn beneath rose sky,
I'll sail to Jiangling ② thousand a mile off a day.
The monkeys on the either bank cry after cry,
My boat's left many a mountain 'hind on my way.

---

① **Badi City** an ancient town located in nowaday Fengjie County, Chongqing Municipality.

② **Jiangling** the present Jiangling County, Hubei Province.

与夏十二登岳阳楼[①]

楼观岳阳尽，
川迥洞庭开。
雁引愁心去，
山衔好月来。
云间连下榻，
天上接行杯。
醉后凉风起，
吹人舞袖回。

① 岳阳楼：坐落在岳州郡治西南，今湖南省岳阳市西门城楼。西临洞庭，左顾君山。

Ascending Yueyang Tower① with Monsieure Xia②

The whole hue of Yueyang City heaves in sight,
The river from afar runs into the Lake③ wide.
A swan flying to south takes away my sorrow,
As in the mouth of mountain, the moon hangs low.
We seem to stay in an inn amid the white clouds,
As in the heav'n, passing the wine cup, we carouse④.
After I get drunk, springs up the cooling breeze
That fluters our sleaves while we are on our home ways.

---

① **Yueyang Tower** a tower built in Yueyang City, Hunan Province.

② **Monsieure Xia** a friend of the poet.

③ **the Lake** the Dongting Lake.

④ **We seem to stay in an inn amid the white clouds, / Passing the wine cup, we in the heaven carouse** These two lines exagrates that Yueyang Tower is exceptionally high.

长相思二首（其一）

长相思，在长安。
络纬[①]秋啼金井阑[②]，
微霜凄凄簟[③]色寒。
孤灯不明思欲绝，
卷帷望月空长叹。
美人如花隔云端。
上有青冥[④]之高天，
下有渌[⑤]水之波澜。
天长路远魂飞苦，
梦魂不到关山难[⑥]。
长相思，摧心肝。

① 络纬：蟋蟀，又称莎鸡、织娘。
② 金井阑：装饰华美的井栏。
③ 簟：供坐卧用的竹席。
④ 青冥：青色天空。高天：一作“长天”。
⑤ 渌：清澈。
⑥ 关山难：关山难以跨越。

Ever Yearning (Two Poems, No. I)

Yearing for my beloved who in Chang'an stays.
In autaumn, crickets whine by the balustrades,
Though light, th' frost's rigid, getting my bed cold.
The lone lamp is dim, I'm dying to miss my belo'ed,
Raising the screen, I gaze at the moon and sigh.
My sweet who's a beauty as flower in clouds high.
Above is so vast a firmament azure,
Below is th' clear river with billowing breaker.
I'm lost in a re'erie of her 'cause she's far cry,
My lovesick heart can't fly over the Mount Pass high.
So pining for her that lost in bro'en heart am I.

少年行二首（其二）

五陵[①]年少金市[②]东，
银鞍白马度春风。
落花踏尽游何处，
笑入胡姬[③]酒肆中。

① 五陵：指汉代高帝的长陵、惠帝的安陵、景帝的阳陵、武帝的茂陵、昭帝的平陵所在地，也是当时豪门贵族聚居地，这里代指家居长安的后门贵族之家。

② 金市：一般指长安西市。一说洛阳三市之一。

③ 胡姬：泛指当时西域少数民族的少女。当时长安多有胡人开酒肆者，店中有胡姬歌舞并侍酒。

Song of Lad (Two Poems, No.II)

A noble lad who lives on th' east of Gold Fair
Rides white horse with silver saddle, face in shine.
Where will he go aft a tour for flower?
To a tavern where Tartar maids serve wine.

渌水曲

渌水明秋日[1]，
南湖[2]采白蘋。
荷花娇欲语，
愁杀荡舟人。

① 日，一作“月”。
② 南湖：庭湖。

Song of Clear Water

The bright sun shines over the clear water,
A lady picks white lemna in th' South Lake ①.
Lotus blooms are so fair as if were to utter,
The oarslady be much woeful they make. ②

① **South Lake** i.e. Donting Lake.

② **They make the oarslady be much woeful:** It implies that the fair oarslady is jealous to the lotus blooms.

秋　思

春阳如昨日，
碧树鸣黄鹂。
芜然蕙草[①]暮，
飒尔凉风吹。
天秋木叶下，
月冷莎鸡[②]悲。
坐愁群芳歇，
白露凋华滋[③]

① 蕙草：香草名。俗名佩兰。
② 莎鸡：蟋蟀，也称织娘、络纬、络丝娘等。
③ 华滋：繁盛（指花草）。

Meditation in Autumn

It was clear spring days of yester[①],
And orioles in green trees were singing.
But orchids amain turned wither'd,
Chilly winds are ceaseless blowing.
In th' autumn, leaves of the trees shed,
And grigs miserably 'loud whine.
I sadly sigh that flowers fade,
In white dews, the flora decline.

① **Yester** here not referring to the day before today, but to the days of spring passed not long ago.

春 思

燕[1]草如碧丝，

秦[2]桑低绿枝。

当君怀归日，

是妾断肠时。

春风不相识，

何事入罗帏？

---

① 燕：周代诸侯国名。在今河北北部和辽宁西部。这里代指位于北方的边疆，诗中女主人公的丈夫在此戍边。

② 秦：周代诸侯国名。位于今陕西大部和甘肃东部。这里指诗中主人公的家之所在地。

Yearning for My Beloved in Spring

Grasses in Yan ①, th' frontier, are like green threads fine ②,
Mulberry sprays in Chin ③ grow lushy to weep ④.
I'm lost into bro'en heart 'cause for thee I pine,
At the moment thou mayst yearn for home in deep.
The spring breeze! Why do you pull my bed screen
And break in amain? I never know you e'en!

---

① **Yan** a name of an ancient state in Zhou Dynasty. Here referring to the frontier where the husband of the protagonist garrisons the border.

② **fine** here meaning thin.

③ **Chin** the region where the ancient Chin State was located and it's the place in which the protagonist's home lies.

④ **weep** here meaning that the branches droop (especially gracefully) , also implying the progtagnist's gloomy heart.

子夜吴歌四首（其二）

镜湖三百里，
菡萏发荷花。
五月西施采，
人看隘若耶。
回舟不待月，
归去越王家。

Song of Wu State (Four Poems, No. II)

The Mirror Lake ① stretches for hundreds a mile,
Where lotus blooms far and wide burst into smile.
The Beauty Xishi ② in June picks the flowers
In Ruoye Stream ③, drawing a swarm onlookers.
Her boat has returnèd ere the moon's rising,
She has been received to th' Palace of Yue's King.

---

① **Mirror Lake** a lake located to the sourhwest of Shaoxing, Zhejiang Province.

② **the Beauty Xishi** a fair, in ancient times. She became a maid of honour in the Palace of Yue's King, Goujian, who later offered her to Fuchai as a honey-trap.

③ **Ruoye Stream** a stream runs in Shaoxing, Zhejiang Province, flowing into Mirror Lake.

劳劳亭

天下伤心处，
劳劳送客亭。
春风知别苦，
不遣柳条青。

The Laolao Bower

The haunt that makes one lost into bro'en heart
Is th' Bower ① where to see off his friends who 'part.
Spring breeze urges not willows to turn green ②
'Cause it knows better that parting is pain.

---

① **The Bower** referring to Laolao Bower where one used to see off his kith and kin..

② In ancient China, one used to break a green willow twig to present his friend who part with him when he see the friend off..

江南春怀

青春几何时，
黄鸟鸣不歇。
天涯失乡路，
江外老华发。
心飞秦塞云，
影滞楚关月。
身世殊烂漫，
田园久芜没。
岁晏何所从？
长歌谢金阙。

Meditation in Spring in River-South ①

How long will last the gaudy spring?
Yellow birds ② are ceaseless singing.
I wander at th' south end of sky,
My hair turned white in th' alien far cry.
To my home my heart flies with clouds,
My shade still lingers' neath th' moon in south.
For my whole life I've roved here and there,
Which makes my farm field be left bare.
What can I do in my years late?
I' ll, singing' loud, waive th' desire for Gold Gate ③.

---

① **River-South** referring to the south of the Yangtze River.

② **Yellow birds** orioles.

③ **Gold Gate** the gate of imperial court. Here is a metaphor for the officialdom for which the poet ever pursued during his previous life.

夜下征虏亭

船下广陵去，

月明征虏亭。

山花如绣颊，

江火似流萤。

A View of Conquest Tower beneath the Moon

I sail my boat towards Guangling City,
Conquest Tower stands beneath the moon bright.
Hill flowers look like cheeks of a beauty,
Like fireflies is many a ri'er boat light.

送韩侍御之广德

昔日绣衣何足荣？
今宵贳酒与君倾。
暂就东山赊月色，
酣歌一夜送泉明[①]。

① 泉明：（陶）渊明。

A Farewell to Censor Han① for Guangde

How glorious in th' past were you in noble livery!
To carouse with you 'night I buy wine up tally.
On th' East Hill we for the moment borrow moonlight
To bid Quanming② a foy, we sing and drink a whole night.

---

① **Censor Han** i.e. Han Xin who was once a censor in the court but now he's relegated and will live in seclusion as Tao Yuaning, a hermit in Jin Dynasty. The poet uses Quanming to substitute for Han Xin.

② **Quanming** i.e. Tao Yuanming, here is a substitution of Censor Han. According to the rule of English language, it is better to use the second person "you". But in Chinese, sometimes the third person is used to substitute for the second person or even for the first person.

王昭君二首（其二）

昭君拂玉鞍，
上马啼红颊。
今日汉宫人，
明朝胡地妾。

Wang Zhaojun[①] (Two Poems, No. II)

She whisks the jade saddle with remorse[②],
With tear stains on cheek, she mounts her horse.
She's a concubine of Han's Palace now,
But missis of Tartar's chief tomorrow.

---

① **Wang Zhaojun** a peerless beauty and the concumbine of Emperor Yuan, Liu Shi of Han Dynasty, she was later bestowed, as a missis, to the Chief of Tartar regime so that its aggression could be avoided.

② **remorse** sadness, woe.

紫藤树

紫藤挂云木[1]，
花蔓宜阳春。
密叶隐歌鸟，
香风留美人。

① 云木：高耸入云的大树。

The Wisteria

Wisteria climbs the wood lofty,
Fair's its vine and flower in spring.
Amid its dense leaves birds're singing.
Its balm infatuates the Beauty.

怨 情

美人卷珠帘，
深坐[①]颦蛾眉。
但见泪痕湿，
不知心恨谁。

① 深坐：长久坐。

Resentment

The fair rolls up the pearl-made blind
Aft she's sat for long with frown'd brow.
Tear stains on her face you still find,
Whom does she so resent with woe?

送张舍人之江东

张翰江东去，

正值秋风时。

天清一雁远，

海阔孤帆迟。

白日行欲暮，

沧波[①]杳难期。

吴洲[②]如见月，

千里幸相思

---

① 沧波：这里喻指相隔千水万山，距离遥远。

② 吴州：三吴地区，也指扬州。

Seeing off Monsieur Zhang① to the East of the River

You will fare for the east of the River②
While the autumn wind is roughly blowing.
A swan afar flies in the skies clear,
Your sail is reluctant to start leaving.
Your day's journey is delayed to th' even,
We won't meet in a time 'cause of far'way.
When th' Moon in Wuzhou rises in heaven,
Trust my yearning for you on Her I may.

---

① **Monsieur Zhang** a high-place official whose surname was Zhang. His name was remained unknown. Here the poet used the official title of Jin Dynasty to substitute for Monsieur Zhang.

② **The River** the Yangtze River.

夜宿山寺

危楼高百尺，
手可摘星辰。
不敢高声语，
恐惊天上人。

Staying a Night in a Hill Temple

Lofty is th' tower that scrapes the sky,
Ascending it, pick a star might I.
Not speak a word aloud I dare even,
Lest I scare those who live in Heaven.

自　遣

对酒不觉暝，
落花盈我衣。
醉起步溪月，
鸟还人亦稀。

Drinking Alone for Relaxing

’Tis getting dark while I’m drinking alone,
Blossom petals fall upon my attire.
I walk along the stream that mirrors th’ moon,
Behold few souls on ground and birds in air.

横江[①]词六首（其五）

横江馆前津吏迎，
向余东指海云生[(9)]。
郎今欲渡缘何事？
如此风波不可行！

① 横江：横江浦，古长江渡口，在今安徽省和县东南。

The Hengjiang River (Six Poems, No. V)

Th' dockmaster of th' ferry warmly greets me,
He points to east where clouds rise o'er the sea:
"Why do you hurry to cross the river?
You can't sail 'cause of rough wind and breaker."

送 别

水色南天远，
舟行若在虚。
迁人发佳兴，
吾子访闲居。
日落看归鸟，
潭澄羡跃鱼。
圣朝思贾谊，
应降紫泥书。

Seeing off the Relegated Who Pays Me a Visit

Boundless is th' river's hue in south for which you fare,
Your boat sails as if she floats in the void air.
Though relegated, you're high-spirited for poetry,
Visiting me when I live a life leisurely——
To view birds who return their nest while th' sun's setting,
And behold in the clear pool the fishes' leaping.
The emperor pines for those like Jia Yi, th' great brain,
You'll get th' imperial edict to be promot'd again.

春 怨

白马金羁辽海东[①]，
罗帏绣被卧春风。
落月低轩窥烛尽，
飞花入户笑床空。

① 辽海东：这里代指边疆或前线。

Resentment in Spring

My swain fights in frontier, riding white steed with gold bridle,
Cover'd with silk quilt, I sleep in bedcurtain as breeze blows.
The moon sets low, through my window peeping the bournt-out candle,
Jeering at me lone in bed are th' petals flying 'to windows.

对　雨

卷帘聊举目，
露湿草绵芊①。
古岫②藏云毳③，
空庭织碎烟。
水纹愁不起，
风线重难牵。
尽日扶犁叟，
往来江树前。

① 绵芊：指草木像丝绵那样柔软、薄弱、纤细的样子很茂盛。
② 古岫（xiù）：古老神秘的岩穴或石洞。这里指幽谷。
③ 云毳（cuì）：本意指毛发，表示云朵清淡、稀薄、朦胧的样子。

A View of Raining

I roll up th' curtain 'far to stare:
The grass in dews grows lush and fair;
Clouds linger in the deep valley,
The dim haze haunts the yard lonely;
The pool ripples as if scatters my woe,
The winds once a while fiercely blow;
An old peasant plows th' field all day,
And shuttles by many a strand tree.

晓　晴

野凉疏雨歇，
春色遍萋萋。
鱼跃青池满，
莺吟绿树低。
野花妆面湿，
山草纽斜齐。
零落残云片，
风吹挂竹溪。

Clearing Up in Dawning

The rain over the weald has ceased,
The spring hue far and nigh increased.
Fishes leap in th' pool being in o'erflow,
Orioles sing in the tree green and low.
Th' flower's like th' tender face of fair,
The hill grass leans 'skew in order.
A few of clouds, as the winds scream,
Hang o'er lush bamboos by a stream

九日龙山饮

九日龙山饮，
黄花笑逐臣。
醉看风落帽，
舞爱月留人。

Attending th' Fete in Dragon Hill on Double Ninth Day

I 'ttend th' fete in Dragon Hill on Double Nineth Day
Yellow flowers laugh at the relegated man.
Being drunk, I care not my hat that's blown away,
The moon's so charming as if asked for me here stay.

览镜书怀

得道无古今，
失道还衰老。
自笑镜中人，
白发如霜草。
扪心空叹息，
问影何枯槁？
桃李竟何言，
终成南山皓。

Meditating While Looking into Glass

One who adheres to justice will be eternal,
One who observes unjustice must be mortal.
I myself laugh at the man in the glass[①],
My white hair is indeed like th' frosted grass
Searching my heart, I, in vain, deeply sigh over:
What on earth cause my hair gravely wither'd ?
If one's distinguished as peach bears rich fruitage,
He'll, as th' old wits in th' South Mountain, be a sage.

---

① **the man in the glass (mirror)** of course it's the poet himself.